Silent Chaos of J31179

A Redemption STORY

Maria Green

CONTENTS

DAILY DEVOTIONAL

FOREWORD
By Barbara Potter

I met Maria Johnson Green in 2019 while she was at the Bradenton Bridge Transitional Center attending the Evangelism Explosion Level 2 class I was leading. As soon as I met Maria, I knew she was someone special. She is someone God has singled out to be a mighty warrior in His Kingdom. He has blessed her with extraordinary communication skills. It will be interesting to watch her grow over these next few years, and see where the *Lord* leads her. I know He has big plans for her life. She has surrendered her life to the *Lord*, and He has big plans for her. She listens to His voice. She studies His Word for her own counsel. He has placed in her the ability to reach people in teaching the Word, leading people to Christ, comforting the hurting, and encouraging the discouraged. She is amazing, all the while keeping a servant's heart. Maria has overcome tremendous obstacles in her own life and continues to face trials and tribulations, however, she keeps her eyes on Jesus and continues to move forward as the Holy Spirit guides her. May God bless her and her family abundantly and do mighty things through her obedience to Him.

PREFACE
By John Patterson

In 2016, I was working as a counselor at a prison work-release when I encountered Maria Johnson Green. Maria had only been at the center for a few weeks and already had a reputation for questioning everything. She was unrelenting, requiring explanations that made sense to her and aligned with her Christian faith. With a reputation as a difficult client, she was reassigned to my caseload when her counselor left. Because of Maria's reputation, I dreaded having to complete a psychosocial assessment. I reluctantly sat down with her for an hour, fully expecting to be interrogated and told there was nothing we could do for her. However, in that short time, I listened to her questions and saw she wasn't being difficult just to be difficult. Maria was so committed to her walk with the Lord that she wanted assurance that our program wouldn't ask her to compromise her newfound faith. I distinctly recall walking out of my office after that first hour-long meeting and telling my clinical supervisor "she may be the one." There is a saying that "Jesus lives in prison" because when people go to jail, they claim to find God, and when they get out, they seem to lose Him. The number of people claiming to have found God is so numerous, it essentially feels insignificant.

The prison culture ostracizes those who refuse to live by the code of the streets. An inmate who doesn't engage in immoral, unethical, or illegal activities is viewed as a threat. Doing time while staying true to Christian principles is incredibly tough. It was a struggle for Maria and it's sad how she was treated. In a strange juxtaposition of roles, it was Maria who comforted me, reminding me that "no weapon formed against me shall prosper" and that "if God brought me to it, He will get me through it." After my first meeting with Maria, I knew she was different. Rarely do you ever see a person of true faith, in or out of prison, and when you do, you recognize them immediately. Maria was one of only three such people I have recognized in my entire career. I wish I could claim credit for the amazing person and powerful speaker she has become, but we both know there is only one who has that power, and that one is God.

Maria's journey touched me, and I know that her story will touch all that hear it. From the depths of poverty as a child in Mississippi, to speaking to Sarasota's elites, her life is a living testimony to the power of God. I am excited to see where she goes next and know that more will be revealed, as she reminded me so often, "in His time, not ours."

FOREWORD TO
Chapter One
By Shana Green

"There is not one experience, no matter how devastating, no matter how tortuous it may appear to have been, there is nothing that's ever wasted. Everything that is happening to you is being drawn into your life as a means to help you evolve into who you were really meant to be here on Earth. It's not the thing that matters, it's what that thing opens within you."
—Oprah

I am so proud of my childhood best friend, Maria. We had so much fun as kids together through our many playdates and sleepovers. We have always lifted each other up. Our friendship helped overshadow things that were happening around us and I am truly thankful for meeting her. She has been through many ups and downs in life but has come out of life's challenges victorious. By putting her trust in God, Maria was able to live the truth of Romans 8:37, "Yet in all these things we are more than conquerors through Him who loved us." I hope that you will enjoy this book and that it will inspire you to push forward and live the best life God has for you.

CHAPTER
One
Born to Live

Before one can truly know themselves, they must know He who created them. But, if you didn't realize you were "created," why would you seek a Creator?

> *Before I formed thee in the belly I knew thee; and*
> *before thou camest forth out of the womb I*
> *sanctified thee, and I ordained thee a prophet*
> *unto the nations.*

—JEREMIAH 1:5

I was born to live, yet I lived to die. I lived by Y.O.L.O (You Only Live Once), but who am I? That's a question I struggled with for most of my life. As a little girl, I dreamed of becoming this highly sought-after lawyer who would fight for innocent lives that were not fortunate enough to hire a decent attorney. I dreamed of taking the money I would earn as a lawyer and moving my family from the impoverished town of Hazlehurst, Mississippi to a better place.

For some odd reason, I have always felt responsible for

my family, even though I was the youngest of the three. Life was hard growing up in Mississippi. My family of five lived in a school bus pushed back into the woods. As other kids got off the bus and ran home to their houses, we got off the bus and ran to the "Magic School Bus," our home and our safe haven. Most kids grew up smelling delicious home cooked meals from their well-suited kitchens; me, on the other hand, smelled red beans and rice from pots outside, sitting on bricks. My mother cooked meals for us daily on a make-shift stove that was nothing more than two bricks with a refrigerator rack laid across the top and a fire underneath. Believe it or not, those were some of the best meals I had. We didn't always live in a bus. For a while we lived in a mobile home that was being torn down and sold to a junkyard for scraps. There were no lights, no water, no stove, no bathroom, or tub. But that was our safe haven.

My mother worked at a nursing home in Hazelhurst, Mississippi. In the evenings, she would feed dinner to all the residents, and if there were leftovers, she would bring food home to us. Some nights this was our only option for dinner. My brother, sister, and I waited long hours for Mom to finish work just so we could eat. This was all we had, and we were grateful. In those moments, our dinner of leftovers was just like the Campbells' soup commercial: *"Mmm, Mmm Good!"* To her credit, my mother always provided, and her strength was remarkable.

None of us get to choose where we are born or what family we are born into. It's fair to say that my childhood was filled with a lot of curveballs that were never knocked out of the park. Most of us know stories about less fortunate kids in Africa, and our hearts go out to them. However, I always remember wondering, "What about me?" For the basic need of water, my mother left buckets outside to catch rainwater. Then I watched her use her t-shirt to strain the tadpoles out of the very water we would drink, bathe in, and that she would cook with. So, yes, what about me? Didn't people see that we were suffering? Didn't people see us starving? Did anyone in the world care? But wait, it wasn't just us. Most of my family were poor, and many African Americans were poor, as well. They all looked just like me —just like us —just like my family.

I grew up thinking that life for my family was pretty "normal," especially for those living in Hazlehurst, Mississippi. Maybe I didn't have it so bad after all. Why would I actually want to be different? Who did I think I was? Did I think that I would make it out of this impoverished town and grow up to be somebody? Did I really believe I would graduate from high school and become a lawyer? What in the world was I thinking, pondering these unrealistic dreams?

Have you ever been in a place of despair where you have no hope? Have you experienced days and nights filled with mourning, toiling, complaining, and total hopelessness?

Man who *is born of woman, Is of few days and full of trouble.*

— JOB 14:1

I felt like this for many years. I was suffering in bondage to the failures and disappointments that came from unfulfilled dreams. These vacant dreams coupled with the fact that I would never go anywhere in life or become anything left me feeling hopeless. Sometimes I wondered what made me think life would be any different from my upbringing. Who told me to have hope in the first place? What was "hope," anyway?

As a child, I felt trapped in Mississippi, even during the summer. While most kids enjoyed a break from school, my siblings and I continued to go every single day, just for food. We enjoyed *Feed the Hungry*: a program created by the government for less fortunate families that was hosted at our local school. School was open all summer long providing meals on a daily basis to kids like us. My sister, brother, and I were guaranteed at least one meal a day, that way, and yes, that made my summers quite exciting.

Along the way, I encountered mocking from the other kids that only went up to the school to link up with their friends. I experienced mean girls pointing out my dirty socks. Still, though, I looked forward to a good meal, then getting off the bus and running into the woods to what I called home.

Yes, life was great and promised me a bright future. If I could just look up and take my eyes off my circumstances, *I would be ok*. If I could just see the best in every situation, *everything would be ok*. I wanted to believe I would make it out to a better place. Could I train my seven-year-old mind to see the beauty and possible outcomes? Could I make it out? Maybe I could push myself a little harder, go a little stronger, study even more. I wanted to believe my efforts would have a direct impact on my future. When failure occurs, we evaluate our efforts and try to understand the true cause. We always wonder "if only this" or "if only that." And in these moments, there are some hard truths we must face.

For many of us, there is family dysfunction hidden inside our precious DNA. There are so many generational curses passed along from one generation to the next. There are so many outcomes we simply cannot change, even if we wanted to, simply because family DNA was engraved and instilled in our bloodline. Because of that very reason, my mom and dad fought often, but I don't mean yelling and screaming. I mean the bloody noses, teeth being knocked out, punches to the face, and swollen jaws type of fighting.

My father always had his "best friend" with him. His first name was Seagram's; last name was Gin. He carried him everywhere he went. Kept him closer than a blood brother, smack dab in his back pocket. His relationship with Mr. Gin soured his attitude and he was often angry, taking it out on my mom, brother, and sister. I didn't understand! I didn't understand how someone I loved could be so mean to my mother. He never struck me, but I still felt the pain of those closest to me. I was equally troubled and confused. Why did he want to hurt them? Why would he make them bleed? Why didn't my screaming stop him?

Why? Why? Why?

Can't he see that we are already in a difficult situation? Can't he see how it hurts me so to watch them suffer? Doesn't he understand how this wounds my mother? As a seven-year-old, how much more suffering could I take? But wait...I love my father; he is everything to me. He is "my Daddy." I would see him and run to him saying, "Hey, my Daddy," as if he wasn't anyone else's father, but mine. But this didn't stop the suffering and I still didn't understand why.

One day I discovered something that helped me understand my father. I learned that he was simply repeating the behaviors of *his own* father. My grandfather beat my grandmother, and so it goes. My dad was only doing what he had been taught. Generational curses are real. They actually do exist, but these generational cycles need to be broken. Oftentimes we find ourselves recreating an atmosphere that feels familiar to us. We find ourselves in the very same cycles that left us feeling broken, naked, and afraid—where there is no way out, no assurance of success, no opportunity for happiness. We find ourselves wandering through revolving doors and committing insane acts because we can't find a way out. We feel stuck, unable to make wise decisions or identify wise choices. We are stuck in the generational "Tag, you're it!" game. Parents pass down hideous traits and harmful behaviors to their children, from one life to another, year after year. But why? Why do we repeat the same patterns?

As I got older, I saw generational curses taking root in my own life, repeating some of the same cycles. I, too, found myself in a relationship that involved fighting, and more fighting. I, too, found myself clinging to a best friend called "Seagram's." I, too, found myself hoarding food, finding all the free food lines. Unfortunately I was too foolish to recognize the patterns. This left me trapped, sitting in whatever insanity it had to offer me. I was caught in the generational curse and couldn't break free. Sadly, I didn't realize my need to break free because this insanity was my "normal." I couldn't even imagine what "different" or "better" looked like.

In my mind, I think I missed some cognitive development as a child. Crucial skills sets that we all develop, as early as age three, enable us to reason, make wise decisions, and make sense of the world around us. These cognitive skills enable children to develop intellectually so they can react and interact with the environment that surrounds them.

I got my depiction of the world from my favorite television shows like *Sister, Sister* and *The Cosby Show*. However, the world around me looked very different. My father was *not* like Dr. Huxtable, nor were the relationships with my siblings like those of Sondra, Denise, Theo, Vanessa, or Rudy. My observations stretched from those model families on TV to my own family's insanity where neither extreme was ideal. No matter where I turned, nothing helped me make sense of my world. Little did I know, my circumstances were about to change.

In September of 1999, when I was thirteen years old, my mother gained enough courage to run. This was a first for me, but it would not be my last time on the run. I have vivid memories of my mother telling me to get up because it was time to go. The sound of her shaky voice scared me, and once again, I didn't understand. My mom, my sister, and I packed our belongings into two suitcases—whatever we could fit—and then headed to the bus station. Along the way, lots of questions were rushing through my mind. I eventually asked in a quivering voice, "Mom, what is going on? Where are we going? Where is dad? Where is my big brother?" In those moments, I was so afraid, that even to this day, thinking about it brings me back to all the uncertainties and dark memories of that day.

Eventually my mom told us we were moving to Florida

to live with Aunt Gloria, Mom's younger sister that I had met a few times. For a minute I got excited because she was definitely my favorite! Then I felt sad because I missed my brother and my dad. My brother, who is just a year older than me, was—and still is—my best friend. At the age of fourteen, he was tired of being beaten by my dad and ran away from home. We had no idea where he was, and during his absence, my heart suffered deeply. Gosh, this was a lot to process! I had no idea what to expect living in a new place, with new people, without my dad and brother. It was like my whole world had changed overnight.

We finally made it to Gainesville, Florida. My father had no idea where we were, but no doubt, he was looking for us. Only a few close family members knew our whereabouts and they wouldn't dare spill the beans. They wanted us to get away and supported my mother's decision to leave. I guess it didn't matter that I loved my father and wanted to be with my brother. For reasons I could not understand, my mother uprooted us from everything we had known and left my brother behind. This decision felt very impulsive. What I couldn't see at the time was how much strength it took for my mother to run. Ultimately, she wanted to give us a better life, no matter what the cost. It took miraculous strength for her to leave an unhealthy relationship and a place she called home.

Strangely I found myself wanting to return home, missing my sense of "normal." In Gainesville, I was living in an apartment with a real bathroom and a real stove. At the age of thirteen, I took a bath in a tub for the first time. This type of living felt so abnormal, so different from Mississippi, plus I missed my father and brother. What I didn't miss, though, was the shame, the embarrassment, and the discontentment of never having enough. But I definitely missed my family. When placed in situations that are beyond our control and above our comprehension, we are bound to take multiple wrong turns before eventually taking the first right one.

When I lived in Mississippi, I always knew what to expect. I knew the people, the places, and my surroundings. In Florida, everything was new, and I felt a sense of fear creep in. My mother had taken us from a dreadful place of poverty, where people glared at our failures, to a place where our future was completely unknown. Isn't it crazy how we want to escape dreadful places, but when we get out of them, fear consumes us? Now, my "normal" was fear of the unknown. As days turned into months, I eventually began to loosen up a little. I embraced my new location, new school, and new friendships. Things were finally looking up for me. People were finally accepting me. I was finally somebody. I thought, "Wow, this is the life!"

Six months into this new chapter, I remember coming home from school one day, walking into the house, and being grabbed by my father. I was so happy to see my dad, but my sister was in dread. Mom finally told him where we were, so he traveled to Florida to be with us. Weeks and weeks passed by, and it seemed like dad had changed. I wanted to believe that separation from us made him become a better man. But then, tragically, this pipe dream was shattered. My sister and I came home from school to find Mom sitting in a corner, bloodied and beaten. Dad was full of rage, holding his best friend's "Seagram's" in his hand. When my Aunt walked in the house and saw Mom's face, she grabbed her revolver, pointed it at my dad, and made him leave immediately.

Just like that, I was fatherless once again. I didn't understand why he came back, only to leave again. I was overwhelmed with intense pain and turmoil inside. I wondered if anyone understood my anguish or even cared! The burden was too heavy for me to carry at such a young age, but I had to survive and find a way through the madness.

As a young teenage girl, I eventually found a solution. I met a girl. I met a girl, smack dab in the middle of a teenage crisis. Smack dab in the middle of me trying to find a way out. Smack dab in the middle of me searching for acceptance. A romantic relationship progressed, and along the way, I was introduced to marijuana. *BAM!* I found the cure to all of life's problems. I had a girlfriend that "loved" me, and I had marijuana that took my pain away. I was living it up; or so I thought. As months—even years passed by—my relationship began to crumble, and marijuana was no longer strong enough to numb the pain. Next thing I knew, cocaine was on the table.

Wow! Cocaine was way better than marijuana. I couldn't feel a thing—mentally, emotionally, or spiritually. Cocaine totally numbed my soul. I used cocaine so much I would skip every single meal, just to get high. The only way to support this new habit was by selling weed, so I started selling drugs to keep a steady supply coming. Every time we made ten bucks, we spent it on a dime bag. On top of that, we partied really hard when we made enough to score an eight ball, costing us about a hundred and fifty bucks. Sadly, this band-aid did not last long. The numbness wore off, and once again, reality set in. The relationship with my girlfriend was extremely toxic. We fought every single day, leaving me completely exhausted. To cope, I got high more often, just wanting to numb the pain. One day it was just too much and sadly, I overdosed. I was out of my mind and totally out of sorts! I took my clothes off and went outside to catch my breath, but that didn't help. In a bizarre sense, all I could feel was my life drifting away. I remember running back into the house and getting into a tub of cold water, and then praying to a God I didn't know. Talking to a God I didn't even believe in. For the first time ever, I spoke to God and told Him I would never use drugs again if he would just spare my life. I told him I didn't want my mom to find me like this; I didn't want her to know her baby girl was struggling with addiction and having relations with a girl. God answered my prayer. He spared my life, but I didn't keep my promise. The very next day, I was getting high again.

Destructive patterns continued to manifest in all aspects of my life. My relationships were plagued with unhealthy behaviors passed down through the generations. I recognized family behaviors that I carried into my relationships. Honestly, bad relationships were all I knew. Fighting meant you loved one another. Clearly, I had a warped depiction of love. I didn't know how to relate well with others, and I definitely didn't understand how to have a healthy relationship. Thank goodness that would all change one day. The same God that knew me when *I did not know myself* would teach me how to have a healthy relationship. God would teach me, through Christ Jesus, what it truly meant to love and be loved, but I didn't learn that until years later.

As time passed, my drug use progressed, and I ended

the relationship with my girlfriend. Almost immediately, I found myself involved with a guy friend. I had no plans to be in a relationship with him, but more so, I just wanted to make her mad. Months passed and this guy friend was still in the picture. I never intended for it to last as long as it did. But to everyone's surprise, we ended up getting married and having three beautiful children.

For me, this meant that at the age of twenty-one, I was a mother of three while dealing with a full-blown addiction. During my pregnancies, I didn't get high as much, but I still got high. My use of cocaine slowed down, but only because I discovered pain pills.

When my first pregnancy resulted in a Cesarean birth, the doctors prescribed 10mg Lortab pain killers. This new pain medication was amazing! I could take pills and not worry about my nose being runny or clogged from snorting coke. This drug was easy to hide, and perfect in so many ways. Cocaine was out; pain pills were in. During that time, my husband was fully entrenched in the streets, selling and pushing dope on every street corner of Lake Butler, Florida. We were both in so deep. We were blind to the empire we were building. An empire that would soon come crashing down.

FOREWORD TO
Chapter Two
By Shelley Taylor

Silent Chaos is a fitting title for this book. I know firsthand because I was there and didn't hear what you were going through. I only heard and saw the things you told me about but was deaf to the chaos you kept inside. It's like being in a room and a crime is committed and everyone there has a different scenario of what happened. I just hope I helped you navigate a little through the chaos. When you counted yourself out, God never did.

CHAPTER
Two
Hiding Behind the Masquerade

For many years, I would describe myself as beauty on the outside, but chaos on the inside. I spent an unbelievable amount of money on hair, eyelashes, and makeup. I chased after anything that would help me mask the pain, the addiction, the fighting, and the despair—all going on inside of me. My efforts to create beauty on the outside, with hopes of masking the chaos, left my soul feeling empty and lonely. I was knee deep in addiction and depression, and yet, I still knew that life was never meant to be this way. I knew I made wrong turns and bad choices. I desperately tried to fix myself. I tried to make myself all right. I tried by wearing the right clothing. I tried by gaining the acceptance of people. I tried by going back to school. I tried to cure my soul with drugs. I tried everything I knew, but nothing worked. As I look back at old pictures of myself, I realize just how much I lived in *"Silent Chaos."* I didn't know how to ask for help. I didn't know I needed help. I didn't realize my life was what I call "Triple O's"—OUT OF ORDER. My normal was all I knew. I labeled my life, *"Silent Chaos,"* because from the outside, everything looked good. But inside, I was dying, and nobody knew it but me.

My heart longed for the American Dream of being the best wife and mom. But instead, I was walking around like a shattered piece of glass. When glass shatters, it breaks into a thousand pieces—and that was me—broken and shattered. I was a little girl trapped inside the body of a woman. I never grew up or healed from all the pain I endured as a child. As a result, I carried all that anguish with me into my own marriage and family. I carried that brokenness into my everyday life. I was beautifully broken, never fully realizing that I was a product of my past. People around me could see it, in fact they tried to tell me numerous times, but their comments never really stuck. I continued to be a beautiful mess, searching for a way out and ways to hide the pain. This led to a place of uncertainty, where I didn't understand my purpose for living. I truly did not know why God even created people if life had no true purpose. If this was all life had to offer, why live?

The miserable atmosphere around me and the lifestyle I was living created a no-win situation where I was caught in a vicious cycle. I hung out with drug users and ate with dope dealers. We were all entangled in the street codes—eating, breathing, living every day in the streets. We sold dope to our own family members, and indirectly, we took food out of the mouths of innocent kids. Every piece of dope a kid's parent bought from us took money directly out of their household. Food money became drug money. My husband and I were too blind to see the unfortunate environment we were creating for our own kids, as well as other dope dealer kids. To get through life, I figured out how to deal with people and responsibilities during the day, so then at night, I could lock myself in the house and get high. I would get as high as the clouds, so much that I could no longer understand myself. It never occurred to me that this was the wrong way. Everyone around me got high. Everyone around me sold dope and ran the streets. From my perspective, this was just the normal lifestyle.

Eventually I reached a place where I could no longer hide. The outward mask slowly faded and the curtains around me began to fall. My nighttime appearance, only seen behind closed doors, was now visible during the day. What happens when you can no longer hide or pretend that you've got your life all together? What happens when the drugs no longer cover the pain—the shame—the guilt? *What happens?* Where do you turn when life is crumbling around you, and everything is spinning out of control? Who do you turn to when everyone around you is stuck in the same normal? *Where do you go?* I had no answers. I had no one to turn to. Church folks were talking about me, telling me I needed to go to Church. Then at the same time, they turned their noses up at me because they knew I was living in sin. I wondered if this crazy cycle would ever end? At this point I was just so tired! I was tired of using drugs —tired of selling drugs—tired of pretending that I was ok. I was completely exhausted! It was time to remove the mask, I had to let it go. *So, now what?*

What's Inside Will Come Out

It seems as if the more I tried to get out, the deeper I got sucked in. My husband and I were so deeply rooted in the streets that many law enforcement officers knew us by name. They knew every vehicle we drove and every move we made. Sadly, we didn't know they knew, so we just kept running the streets. We continued to sell drugs, roll blunts and get high. The more money we made, the more pills I slammed down my throat. At the time, I had no idea what was coming, but major change was on the horizon. I knew my husband was on the radar of Union County's Police Department because of something he did a while back. Years of being on the run was about to catch up with us.

When my husband was seventeen, we welcomed our first son into the world—Jahkwon Green. Just three months later, we got the news that my husband's father had died. Needless to say, he was overwhelmed and distraught with grief. One night he was out driving and wrecked our car into a club. We fled the scene and took off to the nearest city of Jacksonville, Florida, never looking back. We still made the drive back to Lake Butler each month so we could continue to make our drug sales. We found ways to sneak in and out of town between the first and third of the month, filling people with poison, and heading back to the city. This way of doing things went on for a long time. Eventually, the police caught up with us. My husband was arrested and sentenced to sixteen months with the Department of Correction. During his jail term he was granted leave to spend the holidays with his family, with the promise and understanding that he would return on his own.

We knew he had no plans to return to jail. I needed him, and more importantly, our kids needed him. So once again, we picked up and ran, this time to Mississippi. I was much older now and married with children, but sadly my family still lived in poor conditions. We settled in Hazlehurst. We found a nice home and decent jobs, and began to raise our kids. Behind closed doors I was having symptoms of withdrawals, unable to get the drugs I needed. I didn't want my family to see my failures because they thought we had it together. They thought we were different because we dressed like the big city of Jacksonville. Little did they know we were fugitives on the run. Little did they know we were drug dealers and drug users. They had no idea that I was still a slave in my mind, searching for dealers who sold pills. I had to sneak around without being found out and, of course, I succeeded. Once I found a dealer, I sent my husband to pick them up for me. In doing so, I inadvertently introduced him to another dope hole. Strangely, back in the streets we went.

It's amazing how life will take you on backroads to get you on a one-way street in the right direction. Growing up without true guidance left me in a wilderness, looking to the world to learn how to survive. With my upbringing, I never saw success as an option. All I knew was what I knew, and what I knew, l learned in the streets. My mom did the best she could with what she had. I didn't know there was any other way to live because I had nothing to compare it to. Eventually what you know and how you were raised will show its ugly face, good or bad. Whatever is inside of you will come out.

After moving back to Mississippi, I began to think about the dreams and goals I had as a kid. I wanted to get my family out and do better than my parents. Regrettably I found myself stuck in a lifestyle worse than sleeping in a school bus, and now with kids of my own. The very thing I feared had fallen upon me. I would have given anything to go back to the innocent little girl that ate mud pies and played in the woods. I convinced myself I just needed a reset. I thought to myself, if I could just start over, surely, I would get it right the next time. Once again, I prayed to a God I did not know.

"God, I need your help, if you would just help me get out of this situation and lifestyle! I promise God – I will do better the next time. God, I know I lied to you before, but God, IF you are real, I am serious this time. Please help me if you will."

Nothing! I heard nothing! God said nothing! Maybe He said something, and I just couldn't hear Him. Maybe I didn't want to hear Him. Maybe He could see beyond my words and knew my heart. Or maybe, just maybe, He didn't even exist.

Eventually, my husband and I made a bad name for ourselves in Mississippi. Everything we tried to hide ultimately came out. We were deeply entrenched in lawlessness, selling drugs in Mississippi just like we had in Florida. The police raided our house at a time when my husband wasn't home, and thankfully, they let me go. They would come back for my husband, and I knew we couldn't stay. I packed up everything I could fit in a suitcase and left the house. I met my husband on the interstate to make sure the cops were not following me. We picked up our three kids and two dogs and headed back to Florida. Now what? Where would we go from here? What was next?

This would not be the last time we moved and took our family on the run. We went back to Jacksonville, Florida for a few years, but the spot got hot. The cops came after us, so we uprooted again. Enough years had passed, and we thought Mississippi would have forgotten about our altercation with them. We agreed it was safe to move back. We settled down and decided it was time to change. We made an honest effort, but I was still battling addiction and hubby sold marijuana "lightly." We tried to stay low key.

Have you ever reached a time in your life where your resources dried up and everything was a struggle? Without those resources, doing life was no longer as easy as it once was. Have you ever wondered if God is real or why He never answers your prayers? I had those thoughts on more than one occasion. Then I wondered, what if God was answering my prayers all along? Perhaps He was calling me to get out of the chaos and leave the life I built that was totally void of His guidance. What if every incident we encountered was God's warning to us that destruction would come if we didn't turn and truly trust Him. This idea was foreign to me, and it was hard to trust a God I didn't know.

In May 2015, we received a phone call that my

husband's Uncle had passed, and we decided to attend the funeral. We packed our suitcase, got in the car, and headed to Florida for the weekend. It would be a quick trip up and back with plans to return home that Monday. That's *not* how it happened. I was stuck in my chaos and blind to the surroundings. We were on our way back to Florida where my husband's prison sentence was hanging over his head. In addition, I would learn that there was a warrant out for my arrest. These next few months would change my life forever.

Where Am I, and How Did I Get Here?

As we approached the state line, we drove into Florida and saw the sign that said, "Welcome To Florida." Almost immediately my stomach became queasy. I knew we were stomping on dangerous ground. It was very risky to return to Florida, especially on Memorial Day weekend when State Troopers were out in full force. Music was blasting and the kids were in the backseat, singing at the top of their lungs, without a care in the world. If only they knew what was about to happen. As we entered Okaloosa County, I looked in the side mirror and noticed a car following us. Every time we switched lanes, the car followed us. Then it happened—I saw the lights. We were being pulled over! They finally caught up with us. *Oh, no, now what?*

The officer went through all the routine procedures. We both lied about our names, but there was no more hiding. Our identities were found out. My husband had run from his prison sentence, and I discovered there was a warrant for my arrest. When the officer searched our car, he found drug paraphernalia and guns. My husband and I were both arrested, leaving our kids on the side of the road, waiting for the Department of Children and Family to pick them up. The officers charged my husband with possession of a firearm—and possession of drugs. My entire life shattered right in that moment. I felt as if my world had been torn into a million pieces in a matter of minutes. What would I do? How would I make it without my husband and kids? Who would rescue me and get me out of this situation? I had no one to turn to, but strangely, I felt a sense of relief. I was relieved because I was ready to stop running; ready to change; and ready to get off drugs. I couldn't do it on my own, but here I was—in an Okaloosa County jail cell—all alone. I was surrounded by women I had never met who seemed surprisingly happy and content. The weird thing was they were praising God and praying to Him. I didn't understand why. How could they praise God while in jail? Didn't God know they wanted to go home to their families?

The warrant I was arrested on was from Jacksonville, Florida. My mom miraculously bonded me out of Okaloosa County jail that following Monday. She drove miles and miles from Lake Butler, Florida. Unfortunately, though, my husband had no bond for his warrant as he was charged with the drugs and guns found in the car during our arrest. As we drove away from the jail, my heart felt empty. My head hurt. I felt queasy, and to top it off, I had no pills to numb the pain.

I leaned back in Mom's car and lit up a cigarette. As the smoke came out of my mouth, I laid my head back and allowed my heart to cry. My husband was all I knew. How could I just leave him like this? I was devastated. How could I live without him? I knew he was going to prison and there was nothing I could do about it. I couldn't fix "*it*" this time.

What was I to do?

Arriving in Lake Butler, we pulled into my mother's driveway, and I saw "Light" come running out of the house. That "Light" was my children. Finally, they made the pain a little more bearable, however that did not cover up the worry in their eyes that "Daddy" was not here. Gosh, my heart broke for them *again*.

At least Mission One was complete which was to see my kids. Now on to Mission Two: score some pills, coke, weed, or anything to kill this pain! I needed something to ease my withdrawal pains. My body felt horrible! I felt pain *everywhere*, and I just could not stop throwing up. Weeks passed and I realized that I hadn't had a menstrual cycle that month. I thought it was because of stress. I mean, after all, we were stuck in Florida. No clothes. No car, as it had been seized in the search during our arrest.

We were only coming to Florida for the weekend. Everything we owned was still in our home back in Mississippi. We didn't plan to go to jail and get stuck. Although, we knew it was possible. Of course Bonnie and Clyde couldn't get caught — or so we thought.

Our kids had no clothes! *We had nothing*! I thought I missed my cycle due to stress. To be sure, I took a pregnancy test. *Three* tests, to be exact. And each test read positive.

I didn't know how to feel. In 2014, my husband and I paid over $10,000 dollars to have a tubal reversal. I never thought he would be in prison, and I would have to take care of our already three young kids, plus a newborn, by myself.

I grabbed my stomach and cried until I felt empty. I was completely depleted of strength, hope, or happiness. My heart was so hurt. "We have a little person growing inside of me," I thought. But I am alone, on drugs worse than I had ever been before, my husband was in prison, and to add insult to injury, we were homeless. I was going *insane*!

The time finally came for me to go to court in Duval County for the warrant I was initially arrested on. The judge sentenced me to three years of probation. As I drove from Jacksonville to Lake Butler, I felt a bit of pain in my uterus, so I did what I normally did for pain. I ate about four 10 mg Lortabs while never giving any thought about the life growing inside of me. I made it to Mom's and blood poured out of me.

Here we go again, I thought, *losing a baby. Again*! I laid across the hospital bed and watched them remove the lifeless form of our unborn child from my womb. Devastated and in tears, I was so broken.

I left the hospital, alone and afraid, trying to work up the strength to tell my husband that because of my drug use, we lost our baby. What more could go wrong, I thought. I was just put on probation, lost a child, had no money, no home, no clothes, and no drugs to kill the pain.

I took off for a drive and drove straight to Gainesville, Florida. I made a call to my brother-in law and told him I was giving up and needed him to take care of the kids for me. I cried to him and told him I just could not do this anymore.

I hung up the phone with him and drove to the park. As the rain pounded against my windshield, I contemplated suicide. I felt lost, alone, and finished with life. However, I tried one last time to call out to a God I did not know, nor believe in. I cried, "God if you are real, please help me. I *need* you to help me."

Again, *nothing*! I heard *nothing*! I was too weak to take

my own life. I needed to fix this. I needed to make a way. I then remembered I had a checkbook in the glove compartment of my truck. In that instant, I decided to write a check for enough money for food and pills, however I needed someone to cash it for me. I then drove down 13th Street in Gainesville with my kids in the car, and connected with a homeless guy whom I knew needed the money just as badly as I did.

I took him to the Wells Fargo bank and that's where everything started. The teller suspected fraudulent activity and notified the officials. We both ended up getting locked into the bank with a $278.00 check that would send us both to jail. I remember walking out of the bank in handcuffs, my kids screaming at the top of their lungs for mommy. There again, I left them in the care of police officers. Jesus, I needed help. Addiction had taken a toll on my entire life.

As we entered the Alachua County Sheriff's office, I was unaware that there was an open investigation into a group that was going around stealing checkbooks and committing all types of financial fraud. Therefore, we were locked in the bank facility. They thought we were part of that same scheme. Thankfully, the homeless guy was released during his first court appearance. Not me, though. I now had new charges of "Scheme To Defraud a Financial Institution," so bail was set for my new charges.

My mom agreed to pay the bail amount set by the judge and I sat on a bench, waiting for my name to be called. Finally, I heard "Johnson," expecting them to say, "Pack it up." But instead they said, "Johnson, go to booking." I was completely shocked. I didn't understand why I was being called back to booking. My kids were outside waiting for me. My mother had just bonded me out. What in the world was going on? Was I being rebooked? As I approached the booking desk, the officer told me about a second warrant from Duval County—and it was a *no bond* warrant. I was devastated. My heart ached for my kids who were waiting outside for a mother they would not see. I was sentenced to 150 days in the Alachua County jail for the initial warrant. After serving that sentence, I was transported to Duval County in Jacksonville, Florida where the atmosphere was completely different.

Jacksonville was known for its high crime rate, especially murder. The women in this jail had more severe charges, and more drug access. Sometimes we were placed on a twenty-four-hour lockdown. As I settled in again for yet another stay, I began to realize I was in real trouble. Looking around the dorm, days turned to weeks, and weeks turned to months. I began to mingle with some of the ladies in the dorm, explaining my case, and looking for hope from anyone who could offer it. I missed my kids, and I had no contact with my husband in prison.

Once again, I felt like my world was falling to pieces. My heart was so broken. I desperately wanted to see my kids. To touch them, and hear their voices. I desperately missed their smiles. If only I could turn back the hands of time, I would! But here I was—stuck, dead. I was smack dab in the middle of the fight of my life, and I was losing. I was losing badly.

We never realize how our actions directly affect those around us, especially those closest to us. But as an addict, you are not in your right mind. Addicts commit senseless acts out of selfish behaviors and desires of the flesh. Who told me to go into a bank and try to cash a fraudulent check? Who told me to recruit an innocent, homeless man to commit a crime he wasn't even aware of? All I cared about was getting high. I needed pain pills to numb the pain. The homeless man was just an innocent bystander. It seemed like every decision I ever made was motivated out of fear or my need to get high. Now I was in prison, far away from my husband and kids that I was so used to spending all my time with. How dare the world take them away from me? Couldn't the officers see that I was a good person? Couldn't they see that I was just a drug addict crying for help? And where was this God who was supposed to love us? Would this God ever help me?

Eventually my court date arrived. I stood before the judge, shackles on my feet, arms handcuffed behind my back, and wearing an orange jail uniform with J31179 printed where a name should have been. The judge looked at me, said a few words, and then rescheduled my hearing for a month later. I didn't understand what was happening. The "Jailhouse" lawyers told me I would be released to go home. That's *not* what happened, though. I was sent back to my cell, instead. This was the hard-core reality, and there was nothing I could do about it. I was sad, disappointed, and frustrated. On my way back to the dorm, I decided it was time to find the dope dealers of the jail. Certainly it wouldn't be that hard. I knew there were several women with health issues who were issued Tramadol, a low-grade pain reliever. During pill line-ups, these women would hide pills underneath their tongues. When the officer checked mouths to ensure the pills had been swallowed, they couldn't see pills were actually hidden under their tongues. I watched from the other side of the room where I waited for someone to spit out a pill and sell it to me. Truly, I was out of my mind. I still think back to those days and realize now how much I was in bondage to addiction. I had no concept of right living. Who in their right mind would take pills out of the mouths of strangers—especially strangers with diseases who needed that medication? Even then, God had his hand of protection over me.

A month passed by, and the girls gave me hope that I would definitely be released to go home during my next court date. They told me it was likely that the judge moved my date a month later to give me "time-served." I was ready for court so I could be sent home. With optimism and anticipation, I called my mom to make arrangements for her to pick me up. She lived forty-five minutes away, and I wanted to make sure she could be there.

I called my kids and told them, "Mommy is coming home!" I walked into the courthouse that day ready. Ready to finally go home. But that's *not* what happened. The judge studied the evidence against me as presented by the state's attorney. As she read my file, I watched her busy eyes examine the details. Then the judge looked at me and said, "I hereby sentence you to four years in the Department of Corrections, with one hundred twenty days' time-served." My mother screamed loudly as if she had been stabbed with a knife. In that moment, I felt totally *numb*. I was in complete shock. *I fell out.* I literally fell out. The thought of not seeing my kids for four years consumed my mind. How would I survive all those years in prison? What if my kids or my mom died during that time? How could the judge do this? There was absolutely no way I could spend four years in the Department of Corrections. Once again, I suffered a blow to my soul. I was absolutely devastated. I couldn't catch my breath, no matter how hard I tried to just breathe. The look in my mother's eyes was unforgettable.

"God, if you are real, I need you to help me."

Again, nothing. God said nothing. He didn't use a magic wand and set me free upon request. Instead, He made me sit in my failures. Was God really that cruel?

As we headed back to the dorm, the girls were celebrating *for* me. They *thought* I was going home. "Are you going home, they asked?" I could barely speak a word. I threw myself on my bunk and screamed at the top of my lungs. How could I spend the next *four years* in prison? I couldn't wrap my mind, heart, or soul around any of this! I was thirty years old, and I desperately needed help. Ten of us went to court that morning—I was one of two that didn't go home. The other lady was sentenced to thirty-five years, and as soon we got back to the dorm, she started praising God.

As I sat on my bed, I watched a group of inmates form a circle around her and start praying, praising, and chanting to God. Oh, my goodness, that got my attention! It seemed as if everything around me was blacked out except them. I began to feel this calmness that came over me. A sense of peace, and again, relief. I still didn't understand it…yet. As I began to prepare myself for the road ahead, I started thinking that maybe this will be like a second chance. I could get off drugs, and perhaps, live a better life, and one day, become the lawyer I always wanted to be. Weeks passed as I waited for them to call my name for transport. My heart was broken. Broken for my kids. Broken for my mom. Just broken. I needed to be fixed, but who would fix me? I am now at the lowest I have ever been in my life. How in the world did I get here to begin with? Well, there is no where to go now but up.

In life, we tend to find ourselves stuck in the "Woe is me" state. We tend to blame things on others. I mean it's been that way since the beginning of creation right. Adam blamed Eve for the fall. When God had never spoken to Eve, He spoke to Adam, but somehow Adam blamed Eve for his shortcomings. Those are the exact things we do daily. So, when I asked myself, "Where am I, and how did I get here?" I turned inward for the answers.

On June 13, 2016, I felt a kick on my bunk around two in the morning telling me to pack it up. For transport. I was so afraid. My bones were trembling as the tears rolled down my face, this is it, I thought. This is really happening. We loaded the bus as they shackled us together, connecting us to each other, chain by chain around our ankles. "All aboard," one of the officers taunted. I stood crying, waiting to be seated. The windows on the bus were completely blacked out. I had no idea where I was going. I was devastated. Again, with tears now streaming down my face, I asked myself, "Where am I, and How did I get here?" I knew physically I was headed to prison because I broke the law. But this question was by no means physical…I needed to find out the truth…The *true* truth.

> *And ye shall know the truth, and the truth shall make you free.*

> — JOHN 8:32

A New Beginning

*Therefore if any man be in Christ, he is a new
creature: old things are passed away; behold, all
things are become new. And all things are of
God, who hath reconciled us to himself by Jesus
Christ, and hath given to us the ministry of
reconciliation.*

— 2 CORINTHIANS 5:17-18

This is really happening. It seemed as if that ride to Ocala, Florida was the longest ride I had ever taken. I can only imagine how one must feel walking to an electric chair to receive their "Death Penalty." I arrived at Lowell Reception Correctional Facility at the age of thirty on June 13, 2016. I was so afraid I didn't know what to do. I thought I would be the only woman there, as if women didn't go to prison. To my surprise, buses were flowing in from everywhere with women of all races, ages, colors, and sizes. As we are completing the intake process, the guards told us, "You inmates keep your head down. Never make eye contact with us."

It was at that moment that my name changed to "Inmate J31179." It was at that moment the Department of Corrections began to strip me of my identity. I mean, I already had no idea who I was. The next instructions they gave me, would strip me of every bit of self-dignity I had. The next instructions the guards gave me put me to shame. She instructed about ten of us to strip down, line up side-by-side, grab our butt cheeks, bend over, squat, and cough. Multiple women next to me were on their cycles, blood splattered on the floor, right next to me. What in the world is going on here? I cried even harder. I could not believe I was in such a situation and, to make matters even worse, there was nothing that I could do to change it. As the guards led me down the hall, issuing me all the necessary items I needed behind the prison walls. At least all that the State of Florida would provide. I was smothered by reality, devastated, yet in an odd way, relieved. As I laid on the bunk that night. Again, I thought, maybe, this is a second chance for me to get it right. Maybe just maybe. That night, I made the conscious decision that I would not leave this place the way I came in, but I had no idea how I would change. I knew I needed help. Sometimes we find ourselves in situations that seems unbearable, cruel, and unfair. Who can we turn to? Who will hear our cry? No one cares. It's just the way it is, and how in the world could I, too, expect to find help in prison?

My people are destroyed for lack of knowledge:
because thou hast rejected knowledge, I will also
reject thee, that thou shalt be no priest to me:
seeing thou hast forgotten the law of thy God, I
will also forget thy children.

— HOSEA 4:6

God says His people perish due to lack of knowledge, but who would teach me? How would I have even known that that was in the Bible. I was never taught anything about God. Nor was I taught about this man called Jesus that supposedly died for me. And that is all I heard about the first couple of weeks being at the Reception Center: Jesus. *Jesus.*

Who is this Jesus? I needed to know. I needed to find out more information and figure out why He would want to save me. Didn't He see I was in prison? How could He still want to save me? Furthermore, save me from what? No one was after me so, what did I need to be saved from? I remained at the Reception Center for three weeks before two in the morning suddenly comes around *again,* and I feel yet *another* knock on the bed. "Johnson. Pack it up for transfer."

Due to Security breach, you are not allowed to know where you are being transferred to, therefore limiting the possibility of someone jacking the bus and breaking you free. Why was I leaving? I was just getting comfortable there learning the ropes. I met people within those three weeks from all walks of life from murderers to bank robbers to career criminals. But what I remembered most were the Lifers that would never go home yet they worshipped God and spoke to me about Jesus. I was really interested in knowing more about this Man called Jesus Christ. The King of the Jews.

After hours of riding, finally, the bus stopped. As we sat and waited for further instructions, a repeat offender said, "Oh, we are in Quincy," she said, "Y'all, we at Cupcake Camp." I had no idea where Quincy was nor did I have any idea what "Cupcake Camp" meant, but I knew cupcakes were sweet, so maybe this camp was "sweet." They finally unloaded us, two by two. I entered into the facility and was absolutely amazed at how beautiful this place was, there were beautiful flowers everywhere, a garden. I could not believe my eyes as I walked through the breezeway flowers on both sides on me. Right at the ending of the breezeway, my face was met with a ray of sunshine. There was a peace that flowed over me like never before it was then, I said to this God that I did not know, "If you are real, please help me to not leave this place the same way I came in." Looking around me, I could not believe that I was in prison. It looked nothing like the shows on television. I was expecting to see fights, blood, and guts everywhere, but I didn't. I saw flowers and sunshine. I felt hopeful. I had no idea that the next few years of my life would radically change. I mean radically. I was ready. I was ready for change. Inside the dorm, I heard ladies coming from Chapel using words such as bondage. I had never heard that word before, at least not in the streets.

We used words like "hooked" in the streets that means the same as bondage, but I didn't know that. I started asking the house mothers of the dorm questions. I needed to know what *they* meant. Maybe that is what was wrong with me. Maybe I, too, was in bondage. If so, I was ready to let go of everything that had kept me bound for all these years.

I didn't know how, but I was ready to put my best foot forward and learn. I was ready to grab hold of life with everything in me. For my kids, for my marriage, for my family, but mainly, for *me,* because I knew deep down, I *needed* change.

That following evening, my "bunkie," a young lady that slept next to me, invited me to Church. I accepted the invite. I walked into that Church service openminded, open hearted and broken; and I *heard* the words being preached. I *heard* the words. That night July 31, 2016. I gave my life to this Jesus, and of a truth. I haven't been the same since, I knew I would not leave prison the same way I entered. I made that choice myself, before salvation but, what I had in mind was totally different from what God had in mind. I figured I would get my cosmetology license and take a few self-betterment classes.

However God knew, I was still trying to fix myself. I was still trying to gain fulfillment in things. I never got pulled to go into any of those classes. Why? Because God knew I needed a spiritual makeover. He knew I needed to be fixed on the inside, and the inside would manifest on the outside. God knew what I needed. He . . . Just . . . Knew.

He allowed me to come to prison because He knew once He had my full attention, I would hold on to him for dear life. He began to teach me. His people go into captivity due to lack of knowledge.

*Therefore my people are gone into captivity, because
they have no knowledge.*

— ISAIAH 5:13

God used this scripture to shape the course of my life. My question was now, "What do I need to know, God? I am "saved;" now what?"

CHAPTER
Six
Saved, Now What?

I said the prayer, asked for Jesus to come into my life and save me but nothing changed. As a matter of fact I began to go with the flow of the women in the prison. They had girlfriends and were still going to Church. Still stealing out of the "Chow Hall." The very same people that gave their lives to Jesus, as I did, they didn't change. How could this be? How could we not look different? Like the other women that I saw coming in. I thought Jesus made the difference in your life. I thought he would make me better. Stop me from being "hooked" or bound by this devil. By Satan. I didn't realize that *I had to apply myself. I didn't know that I was supposed to seek Him.*

I started going to the Chapel and hearing words such as the "Gospel" of Jesus Christ. Preachers would come from the outside and tell me that I could be free in prison. How could that be? The judge hit the gavel and sentenced me to four years in the Department of Corrections, but these people are here feeding me false hope: That if I accepted Jesus into my life, I could be free. Right, where I was!

*And ye shall know the truth, and the truth shall
make you free.*

— JOHN 8:32

That didn't even sound right. Obviously, they didn't see the fence, or they must have missed the gates when they were walking in, or maybe they *were* just giving me false hope? I signed up for the faith-based dorm because, clearly, I needed guidance, self-discipline, and understanding. I really needed to know about GOD. I needed to know how to be free, and the Chaplin recommended that I sign up for their program. I did.

After weeks of being there, I started hearing words such as "worship" and "praise." I still could not grasp the concept of people praising God *in* prison—it just didn't make sense to me, but I played along.

In faith-based, we were required to attend a certain amount of Church services per month. The more I attended the hungrier I got to know more. I desired a relationship with Jesus. I wanted so badly to be forgiven. The preachers coming in kept saying I had to "repent."

I started going to Chapel more than what was required, and I looked up words such as repent, worship, and praise. I heard words such as the Holy Spirit and salvation, as well as my personal favorite, *forgiveness*. My goodness, this was music to my ears. I needed this, I wanted this, and I was willing to do whatever it took. Whatever was necessary to be forgiven.

God, I started to pray, "Help me, teach me, guide me." The preacher said, "I should ask God to make me more like him." I desired to be *free*. I desired to feel the overwhelming love that came from being saved. I wanted to reap the benefits of accepting Jesus into my life.

It seems as if nothing changes immediately, but if you keep pushing, praying, and persevering, you will soon see that God is real and the Gospel of Jesus Christ has the power to save souls. It is the power of God unto salvation to everyone who will believe. We were all bought at a price. I never understood that because I was never taught it.

The ways of the streets and my corrupted mindset had me bound by the devil and his schemes. I lived in the world without a Savior because I didn't know anyone wanted to save me in real life.

A seed was planted in my life, and it started back in the county jail. God had already illuminated the women before my eyes. Now, it was beginning to make sense; that freedom the preachers had been preaching to me. Months passed and I started to really take this salvation thing serious.

Eventually, I started to change; I could feel it. I will never forget the first day I raised both of my hands up in surrender to God. You see, I would already raise one hand up during praise and worship, but what a difference two raised arms meant to me. I totally surrendered to God. I surrendered to Jesus. I surrendered my life to the Gospel of Jesus Christ.

I didn't know what that would look like, but I would soon find out. I was growing and learning the ways of God. I joined the praise and worship team at the Chapel and was in a place I had never been in before. I was free, y'all! Free in prison! I was free; Jesus had set me free. Glory to God. Then, something happened. In faith-based, there were mentors. Mentors that were appointed by the Chaplin over the dorm. A certain woman they called the "House Mother," simply because they felt she was the most anointed in the prison. However, before prison, she was a preacher. I started to watch her, to look up to her, to idolize her.

She was so worshipped in the dorm to the point that she would have us carrying her books and her belongings from place to place. They would even make her bed up for her. Even the guards respected her. Plus she had family on the outside that kept up with anything she needed. She was exactly what I thought I wanted to be. However, it seemed as if the more I read the Bible, the more *I realized that her ways did not add up to how God said we were supposed to live our day-to-day life.* I was so confused.

Again God, how can this woman that seems to have it all together not be an example of you? God said to me, "I will teach you my ways. No man needs to teach you anything; keep your eyes on me. Focus on me, do not worship people." I asked, "God, why?" Why is He making me do this alone? God, I finally feel accepted among this group of people. Why, God, are you pulling me away again? Can't you see that I need their help?

I was next to become a mentor in the dorm, just awaiting the Chaplin to appoint me. I went to the "House Mother" and asked her what she thought God would use me for. She said, "Oh, you will just be the help." She said, "God will just use you in hospitality." She crushed my spirit. It wasn't what she said, it was *how* she said it.

However, I didn't let the instructions from God, nor her criticism, stop me from wanting to be like her. Until one day when we went to the Chapel, and I watched her buy contraband from a lady on the compound and smuggle it back into the dorm with my own eyes. I was devastated. I didn't know what to do. That night I cried so hard in my bunk. I tossed and turned, confused, crying out to God. God spoke to me and told me to tell the Chaplin what I saw. He said, "She will not believe you, but you must tell her."

God took me to Jeremiah 1:8, "Do not be afraid of their faces: for I am with thee to deliver thee, saith the Lord." I was in awe. Complete and total awe that God would speak to me so plainly, but He did. The next day, I walked into the Chaplain's office to tell her what I saw. She in turn called the entire praise team and their leader in, who happened to be the "House Mother." She denied it, of course.

What happened next was completely beyond me. I was kicked off the praise team and most in the dorm turned against me. I felt alone, once again. What do I do now? If I sign out, they will put me on the "compound" with the "non-saved" people. God, what am I supposed to do now? I had no one. Mom was not able to afford to put money on the phone. My husband was in prison. I had no friends; no one to talk to. I was completely alone. Though, little did I know, I was right where God wanted me. I was still in faith-based and continued to attend Church while dealing with the hate and anger coming from the "Church people" who supposedly had knowledge of God, even though their hearts didn't. Though I didn't understand how they could be like this at that particular moment with my still being such a new follower of Christ.

Different preachers came in, and for the first time, I heard words such as sanctification and consecration. Of course, I immediately ran to the Chapel and found a Bible commentary to look those new words up. Then it finally made sense: I was alone because God was consecrating me. He was setting me apart from sin, and Jesus was connecting me back together with the Father. God was teaching me through this hurtful situation. His true law. And He used them to teach me what not to do. God showed me exactly where I was in Him, and He promised He would deliver me from them in due time. In *His* time.

It is absolutely amazing how God uses the people and places around you to get you to the place He knows you were destined to be. God created us for life. Not just life, but a more abundant life.

*In which time Moses was born and was exceeding
fair and nourished up in His father's house
three months: and when he was cast out,
pharaohs daughter took him up, and nourished
him for her own son. And Moses was learned in
all the wisdom of the Egyptians and was
mighty in words and deeds. And when he was
full forty years old; it came into his heart to
visit the children of Israel and seeing one of the
suffer wrong he defended him, and avenged him
that was oppressed, and smote the Egyptian.*

— ACTS 7: 21-24

God allowed Moses to be removed from his home and grow up in the middle of the world (Egypt). He allowed Moses to gain worldly knowledge. He allowed Moses to see, hear, and feel, firsthand, what his people had to go through under the hands of Pharaoh. I believe Moses had a heart for people since his birth. I believe God allowed Moses to become so powerful before the very people he would have to go back and redeem, because God already knew the thoughts and plans He had for Moses's life. God allowed Moses to be brought up in the very home that He would destroy. Moses gained wisdom and knowledge of Pharaoh and his ways, and God used him to go back to redeem His people and Israel.

But first, God had to establish Moses's identity in him. I looked to the House Mother because I still didn't know my identity in Christ Jesus. I looked to her to tell me who I was, but I didn't let her word be the final authority. Just like Moses. God called us out from the beginning of time.

Saved, now what? Now was the time for me to truly learn of Christ. Now was the time to realize that God had set me apart from the beginning of times, despite my current location or situation. Now was the time for me to realize that, just like Moses would go back to redeem his people. God had called me for such a time as this to use me in unimaginable ways. I was ready to say, "Here I am Lord, use me."

> *Also I heard the voice of the Lord, saying, Whom shall I send, and who will go for us? Then said I, Here am I; send me.*
>
> — ISAIAH 6:8

I often say, "To redeem a thing, one must go through it first." Would I have chosen to go to prison and be away from my family? No, I wouldn't. Not unless I knew God first. But with the mind of the world, I would have never agreed to willingly go to prison. Yet God so loved us that He sent Christ to die for us.

> *And he is the propitiation for our sins: and not for ours only, but also for the sins of the whole world.*

> — 1 JOHN 2:2

Redemption started there. Jesus went through this world. He was tried, tested, and tempted, just as we are. Jesus passed the test. He is now able to stand as our ultimate Redeemer.

Moses also went through tests and trials. Moses was able to stand as our leader. No, he didn't stand perfect like Jesus, but still, he stood. The words spoken by him still lead us today.

I was taught by the world how to live, breathe, and make life make sense. Full of worldly knowledge, yet perishing for the lack of knowledge of God, addicted to Lortabs and Percocets, and not understanding life. I couldn't make life make sense for me, yet God was calling me unto Himself. Like Moses, God knew that once he imparted His truth and wisdom to me, I would run for Him with my whole heart. He knew I would not look back. I would not be like Lot's wife. He knew I would be the salt of the earth.

Don't judge your current situation too soon. Seek God to see what exactly he would have you do, right where you are. Maybe you are in a physical prison. Maybe your prison is mental. Maybe you are stuck by addiction. Maybe you are battling homosexuality, yet you accepted Christ.

Let me give you some advice: be patient. Be patient with yourself. Be patient with God. Be patient with your progress because those that wait on the Lord, shall renew their strength. You will mount up on wings as eagles. You shall run and not be weary. You shall walk, but God will not let you faint. (Isaiah 40:31) Who do you know that plants a seed and stands over it to watch it grow? No one. But they continue to water it, regardless. Likewise, if you have accepted Christ into your life, water the seed he has planted in your heart, in your soul, in your life. Whatever you do, don't get discouraged.

Do. Not. Get. Discouraged.

As months passed, I felt the nudging of the Holy Spirit leading me to sign out of faith-based. I was hesitant—rules were if you signed out of faith-based one would be forced out of the dorm into the compound where the "sinners" were. The "sinners" were the ones not seeking God and still running the "prison streets" using drugs and fornicating with officers. I finally came to grips that the Holy Spirit would *not* let up, so I walked to the Chapel and signed out. Sure enough, I was put on the transfer list to be moved out of the dorm. Days, weeks passed as I waited for them to say "Inmate J31179, Pack it up!" That *never* happened. Instead, God moved the entire faith-based dorm into the compound. I was the only one left in the dorm. Daily I watched God strategically place people in the dorm. People that loved Him and needed to be led and encouraged. He told me in Joshua 5:9, "This day I have rolled away the reproach of Egypt from you…"

That was my scripture reading of that very morning. I

looked around and started to bless God. He had delivered me from them just as he said. Now, I had a choice to go to Church.

He wanted to know that I would serve Him without being forced. God was testing me. I ended up leading that entire dorm. I was there the longest. The officers knew me, and they trusted me. God had made me a leader and there was nothing I could do about it but lead. He wanted to know that I would serve Him without being forced. I had no idea that God was preparing me for my Exodus.

CHAPTER
Seven
The Exodus

"Johnson to Classification." Classification, I thought, for what? Do I have outside charges? Why would I need to go to Classification? I walked along the sidewalk of Gadsden admiring the beautiful flowers. It was such a beautiful place. I finally saw prison for what it was meant to be, it was called the department of corrections for a reason. It was put in place to correct you. Yes, some officers and security guards definitely did not do their job. They were molesting women, brutally beating them, as well as sleeping with them in return for bringing drugs into the facility. But ultimately, the purpose of the facility was to correct. God ordained it. I made a conscious choice to allow that place and God to correct me.

> Let EVERY soul be subject unto the higher powers.
> For there is no power but of God. The powers
> that be are ordained of God.

> — ROMANS 13:1

Finally, I made it to the Classification Officer. She said to me, "Johnson, you are here to sign for pre-work-release." I gave out a huge sigh of relief, but still had no idea what work-release even was. Did this mean I would be released to work? She asked me which facility I would prefer, I chose Bradenton, Florida over Orlando. I could not believe what had just happened. My name was on the call-out for work release, so everyone saw it, including the "House Mother" that had been incarcerated for almost ten years. She had signed for pre-work-release, yet never had the chance to go because "Most people never go to pre-work-release." At least, that's what I was told.

As soon as I walked through the breezeway, her face was one of the first I saw, although we were in different dorms, we all had the same call-out. She looked at me and said, "Don't get your hopes up. Nobody ever goes to pre-work-release." I said "Oh, yeah," and continued walking. God had matured me so much that I knew what type of response she needed.

That night I cried my eyes out. Not because I was going to go to work-release, but because I had just found God. How could he ask me to leave Him? Surely, this was of the devil. Surely, God is not telling me to leave Him here. I was devastated. The next day, I sent a request to Classification refusing the work release transfer. Weeks passed by yet I heard *nothing* from Classification. Finally, during mail call, I received the request back that told me if I refused pre-work-release, I would not be able to go to regular work-release. I still had twenty-nine months left on my sentence.

I did what I knew to do—I prayed. I asked the Lord if it was meant for me to go, to please give me a sign. The very next day, the Chapel caught fire. I could not believe what had just happened, and still today, I am in awe of the way God led me through. I knew God was with me, but somehow in my childlike mind, I thought that if I left, I would leave God behind not knowing that He is everywhere, always. Though I would soon find out again.

Days turned into weeks and then it happened around three in the morning. I felt a knock on my bed: "Johnson, pack it up." This would be my third move in less than a year. I could not believe God was delivering me from prison in just ten months. I cried so hard while I was changing out of my prison uniform. I was in such awe of God and how much He loved me. I will never forget the endless flow of tears and the peace and joy I felt in my soul, not because I was leaving prison, but because *God* was the one guiding my steps. I had never felt so free before in my entire life. I knew that God was with me. I knew I was heading in the right direction.

Take it from me—God will meet you right where you are. There is nothing that you have done in this life that our Lord is not willing to forgive. Let no one tell you that you have gone too far, or you need to play a certain role. If God could save a broken down, undeserving sinner like me, He is waiting and willing to do the same for you.

I was knee deep in sin: a liar, a thief, a homosexual, and a slanderer, completely separated from God. God picked up my pieces, though, and Jesus connected me back with the bishop of my soul, and He is no respecter of person. We are all unique individuals that get sucked in by ignorant teachings and a lack of knowledge being passed down from generation to generation. But I tell you this…the curse breaker lives. The curse breaker is waiting and willing for you to say yes and just repent. His arm is not too short that he can't save you, nor are his mercies replenished. The Grace of God is waiting to cover you right where you are. He is the author, finisher, and perfecter of our lives, but he will not force Himself on us...He didn't force me...Nor will he force you. He is gentle.

I had no idea where I was going, but I knew I did not want to go without God. As the guards loaded me onto the bus, I knew then I was different. My life was not the same. God had honored me in the presence of all who had mocked me. He had delivered me from my enemies. The same God that has been calling you. The same God that created you is the same God that has your back. I mean, I thought I would have to physically die to start over again. Funny thing is if I would have died in the streets, I was going to hell, because I was separated from God. I was spiritually sick, living by the street code and killing myself daily. But God showed me mercy and extended me grace.

Now, my first Exodus had arrived. I was at another bridge. Another bridge to cross. This bus ride would be different from the first few as this time I knew God was the one orchestrating this move. True, He orchestrated the other moves, as well, but I was unaware of His presence. This time I was fully aware. God was personally parting the Red Sea for me. Bridging the gap.

Bridging the Gap

[18]Remember ye not the former things, neither consider the things of old. [19]Behold, I will do a new thing; now it shall spring forth; shall ye not know it? I will even make a way in the wilderness, and rivers in the desert.

—ISAIAH 43: 18-19

After almost five hours of riding on the transport bus, it finally came to a halt. I stepped off the bus to a place that looked like a hotel. It was hurricane season, so the windows were boarded up and the building looked practically abandoned. Immediately a group of women walked out to us. They greeted us with warm smiles and even walked on the grass, which was foreign to me.

In the actual prison, inmates better not dare walk on the grass. Now, here I am in a place where the women are not only wearing regular clothes, but they are walking on the grass. They are friendly, no handcuffs, smoking cigarettes, and all. Where am I, Lord?

As we entered the building, these women gave us

welcome packets. These packets contained cash money with actual coins. I hadn't touched money in over a year, I was so overwhelmed. I was in complete awe of how I was delivered from prison to the place I was in now, pretty much overnight.

Women were working and leaving the facility with monitors on their sides. They were going to Church in the free world. They actually had Publix delivering food. And a lake! There was a lake with turtles and ducks. This place was amazing! Why did God love me so much? Why was He extending so much Grace to me? I didn't deserve this. I deserved to be in prison behind the fence, serving my time. I had committed a crime that I deserved to be punished for. Didn't God see that I was a horrible person? I just could not believe this was really happening. I started to think that I was in the place that God wanted me to be, all along. God was truly showing Himself to me in a way that I could never explain. I didn't feel I deserved this, but God said yes, I did. Oftentimes we read stories in the Bible, and we see how God used imperfect, ordinary people to do extraordinary works.

Although I did not feel worthy to be where I was, God saw fit. The Lord said we all have sinned and fallen short of His Glory, but His arm is not too short that He can't save us right where we are planted. You see, it's because we know our own deep dark secrets, we truly know how deep our sins are, which causes us to feel unworthy.

But know this…you can hide yourself from people, but you cannot hide from God. He knows absolutely everything about us. Every mistake. Every failure. *Everything*. There is nothing hidden from His eyes. He knew we would commit these actions before we ever even committed them, yet he still sent his one and only son to die for us.

God will take our failures and use them for his purposes if we are willing to let go and let Him. The enemy will try to condemn you while Christ is trying to set you free. He who the son sets free, is free indeed. Be mindful of the tactics of the enemy. You see God had just delivered me and set me free, but the enemy was trying to keep me bound by what I knew about my past self. I needed to be delivered from me.

Think about this: who in this world truly knows *all* of your secrets? Who knows those things you are most ashamed of? Who knows those things which were done in the dark and that have never been brought to light? Only you. The enemy will try and use that to condemn you, but know this…God knows it too, and He shall set you free.

I was right where I was supposed to be. Maybe I didn't deserve it, but Psalm 103:10 says, "He hath not dealt with us after our sins; nor rewarded us according to our iniquities." Thank God, He does not treat us as our sins deserve. That's perfect grace and mercy.

Bradenton Bridges of America is the name of the facility where God placed me. After the first week of being there, I learned that before I could go out to work, I had to go through rehabilitation. It was offered at Bridges of America. I would have to complete certain classes and go through recovery-based programs. I was fine with all of that. My problem came when I was told I could not say the name "God."

My world was shattered again…I just could not believe God would put me in a place where I could not say His name after all He had done for me. There is no way I could keep quiet. It was not in me; God had been too good to me.

He was the realest person I had ever met in my life. What in the world did they mean I couldn't say his name? *No, no, and no!*

I immediately went to my counselor and told him to send me back to prison. He asked why? I told him that I would never not speak about God. God did not just give me recovery, God delivered me, and no one — absolutely no one —would tell me not to speak of His name. My counselor did not grant my request. God had given me a counselor that could see through a lot, he would answer me by asking me a question. To find the answer to his question, I would need to look within myself.

Grateful is an understatement to the gratitude I have for this man. God knew I needed someone like him to counsel me. He refused to allow me to sign out, and at this time, I felt like Daniel in the Bible when they told him not to pray to God. In Daniel, Chapter 6, this story can be found. I refused to not speak the name of my Lord. I began to speak of his name more because there was not a demon in hell that would stop me. I knew that the same God that delivered me from the hands of my enemies in Quincy would deliver me here. I knew God had placed me there for a reason, and no one human could move me. God was beginning to bridge the gap. It would be in this place where I would walk out with everything that God had been teaching me. I started to pray and asked God, "Where am I? Lord, why am I here? Father, show me what you would have me do in this place."

When God has his hand on you, nothing and no one can move you. Only you can move yourself out of position. Satan will try everything possible to get you to believe that his works are the works of God. Jesus said his sheep will know his voice and another voice they will not follow.

> *27My sheep hear My voice, and I know them, and they follow Me; 28and I give eternal life to them, and they will never perish; and no one will snatch them out of My hand. 29"My Father, who has given them to Me, is greater than all; and no one is able to snatch them out of the Father's hand.*

> — JOHN 10: 27-29

The job of the enemy of your soul is to steal, kill, and destroy the works of God. I mean, after all, didn't he tempt Jesus by saying, "If You are the Son of God, throw Yourself down. For it is written: 'He shall give His angels charge over you,' and, 'In *their* hands they shall bear you up, Lest you dash your foot against a stone'" (Matthew 4:6). He tempted me by saying, "Surely God did not bring you to a place that you can't say his name," but He was wrong. I stood firm. I stood firm on what I knew God called me to. Months continued to pass. I started hearing words such as addiction, trauma, recovery—words I had never heard before in my life. Codependency, manipulation —those words were never a part of my vocabulary. They were definitely never used in the streets.

We didn't say, "Hey, look at that addict." It was more like, "Look at that crackhead," and that only referred to the people that would sell their food stamps to get high, or light up their pipe in the middle of the streets. I never realized that I was exactly like those "crackheads." I didn't realize that we were all just stuck in addiction. Putting a label on a thing definitely matters. It made me look at life completely different. Thank God that the blood of Jesus not only gives us recovery, but He delivers. He delivered me from addiction and codependency. God was using this program to connect the dots and to bridge the gap to what I had been through throughout my life.

We all have suffered from some type of trauma that caused us to make the decisions we have made in our lives. I grew up around a violent father. I found myself in a relationship that involved violence. I suffered from a fear of lacking…why? Because we never had enough. Not enough food. Not enough water. Not enough time. Love. Encouragement. I have lacked in every way possible, so, that created a fear within me of never having enough. I carried that fear with me everywhere I went. We all have reasons why. Why we end up traveling the roads we travel. Our journey is different from one another.

As time passed, I learned that the founder of Bridges of America was sentenced to several years in prison. God gave him the vision for that facility while he, himself, was serving a prison sentence. It used to be a faith-based facility until He died. The state then took over and tried to take God out. I ended up writing petitions to the daughter of the founder and everything changed. God had His name placed back in the place it originally was meant to be. We were now able to speak freely and testify of His goodness right there. The Lord told me I was standing on holy ground, and because of my obedience, His will was done in that place. It was not easy to have to stand alone again, but God delivered me once again, just as He did before. He gave me favor with the officials.

Obedience will take us places in God. It's not for our Glory. God will share His Glory with no one, nor will he compete with anyone. It is better to obey the Lord than man. I could have made so many different choices in that place, but God had saved me from me and all I wanted was to serve Him. I completed rehab and was now prepared to go out into the free world and find a job. Was I ready?

God placed so many people in my life to lead, guide, and direct me, but it was at The Bridges of America that I truly learned how to be the hands and feet of Jesus Christ. The women He had there waiting for me shaped my life and future. They taught me things I had never known before — how to live and serve the Lord in such a way. They helped me be prepared for exactly what I am doing now, as well as for the next steps that God would have me travel. They encouraged me, supported me, and just down right showed me the love of God in a way that cannot be put into words.

Where there is no counsel, the people fall; But in the multitude of counselors there is safety.

— PROVERBS 11:14

I knew I was safe with them. They counseled me in every aspect of the way.

Plans fail for lack of counsel, but with many advisers they succeed.

— PROVERBS 15:22

God had given me many advisers. They mentored me. Advised and counseled me. God had even given me a mentor who would shape the way I spoke. She taught me how to properly speak and communicate, and she loved the Lord. Praise Jesus, what a difference she made in my life! I will be forever grateful for those that God placed in my life to teach me along the way. The women who came in every single week that taught me how to be the hands and feet of Jesus Christ, they loved me, worked with me, and taught me in and out of prison. God used them to bridge the gap.

As every child needs to be taught how to walk on their own, how to digest solid food and be weaned from breastmilk, God will always put someone in position to teach us, if we are humble enough to accept the leaders and mentors that God has assigned to us. These women had reassured me that I was ready. I was ready for my next step. I had never served God outside of prison before—was I ready for the temptations that would come with the territory? God said, "Yes!"

FOREWORD TO
Chapter Nine
By Linda Spagnolo

When Maria asked me to write a forward for *Silent Chaos*, I pondered where to start. I love speaking about Maria—she is one of the godliest women I know. From the first time I met her, I continuously saw change in her countenance growing and glowing. She is a truth teller, a question asker, and a firm believer in the resurrection of Christ. She is, and I believe always will be, a student of Jesus. As she shares her story with anyone who'll listen, truth and wisdom are infused throughout her words.

As I was coming up on my 8th year of volunteering with Evangelism Explosion Prison Ministry (EEPM), I met Maria at The Bridges of Bradenton (TBB), a women's work-release program in the state of Florida. She really stood out among all the other inmates. It didn't take long for me to sense the Spirit of God dwelling in her heart and mind. Today she is committed to sharing the Gospel of Christ to help His incarcerated Church obtain hope right there where they are, behind bars. Maria shows the reader how God was with her, even when she didn't realize it, directing all her steps—and that even while in prison, a man-made bondage, she was literally free.

My impression of Maria's book is that it will bring light to our incarcerated brothers and sisters—and remind anyone searching for reasons to trust God, that He is *always at work*. Although shackled, Maria was free in Christ while still behind prison walls. And now she wants to tell the world about Him.

This book tells the story of her unprivileged life that God had His hand on since before she can remember. If you have ever struggled in bondage of any sort, this book may relate to your story as well. I truly pray the reader is blessed by this labor of love.

CHAPTER
Nine
God Spoke

God had spoken. He told me I was ready. Obviously, He knew more about me than I did, as I was terrified to go out into the streets again. I had no idea where I was. I had never been to Bradenton, Florida a day in my life. Yet, I was here now. God said it was time for me to serve Him at a different level, a greater capacity. God was about to teach me things that He had never taught me before—new ground and new lessons.

I found a job at a local diner in Bradenton. I worked, came in, taught classes, facilitated Bible studies. Every single Sunday I was allowed to go to Church. God allowed me to go to concerts in prison and give my testimony on live television. One weekend, my kids, whom I hadn't seen in three years, were allowed to attend, all-expenses paid. The rule at the work-release center was that every inmate was only allowed to have one job. But God had spoken. He gave me favor with the officials of the prison. They allowed me to have a second job at Red Lobster. I worked, taught, facilitated, and God was teaching me firsthand how to be a leader outside of prison, while still in prison.

Not one single person on this earth or in this world could ever change my mind about God. He has made Himself real to me. I have tasted and seen what the blood of Jesus Christ can do in the lives of a surrendered individual. When God speaks, no one could ever change His Word. No one can go against the grain of God. I was preparing myself for my final exodus. God was preparing me for the day that I would be released back into the world with no discipline, and without anyone to stand over me, telling me when to get up.

In work-release, we had to wear monitors around our waists and ankles which told us when we were in a place that we were not supposed to be. It was like a human GPS that the officers used to keep tabs on all of their inmates. If we went out of bounds, it would notify the office. They would send a message to the monitor that then told us that we were in an unauthorized area and needed to walk around outside until they could detect us. I called that monitor my "Grace Mobile" because it was by the Grace of God that I was even there. I always did what I was told without complaint or grumbling. I knew that my life was being orchestrated and lead by God. The closer it got to my release date, the freer I felt. I was not sitting and waiting on the date because I was already free. Free right there in prison. This was that true freedom that they preached about. I now preach about that freedom to all those that came after me in prison. God had spoken. God allowed me to teach and preach right there in prison. It was my training ground for the road ahead. God, Himself, was building me up and teaching me. During the last five months, before I was released, I was baptized in the Bridges of America pool, located on the backside by the lake. God said to me, "Those who have received much, much will be required of them."

I worked long and hard to make enough money to relocate my family. I needed to stay around the support system God had given me, and surely, He set me up. God placed some of the most genuine people in my life throughout this journey. I will forever be grateful. Truly, they fulfilled the meaning of visiting the prisoners to set the captives free. God placed a set of women around me that taught me so much. They led me, guided me, cried with me, sent gifts to my family, and helped paid living expenses. The Ministries that God placed at my fingertips taught me how to be the hands and feet of Jesus.

We can never take for granted the people that God places in our lives as a light. When God speaks, we must make sure our ears are open and that our eyes are steadily on the Lord. We all need iron to sharpen us.

As the days turned into weeks, weeks turned into months, and it was now time for me to start searching for a home to relocate my family. Call after call. No after no. Most people did not want to rent to a convicted felon, even though my credit score was decent. I had two steady jobs, plus the entire deposit amount to pay to move into the property, yet, they still said no. I became discouraged. I cried out to God, and He spoke. He led me to a beautiful property on a cul-de-sac on a dead-end street, and lights were even included in the rent. The home was perfect. Although I knew it was God leading me, doubt crept in. I refused to fill out the application because I was tired of getting turned down and judged.

I was a server at Red Lobster and one day I went to work and one of my regular customers came in. She was a pastor and asked, "How is the house search going?" I told her bits and pieces, and I also told her about the one that I wanted. She asked, "Well, did you put in the application?" I said, "No ma'am." She said, "Well, how do you expect God to move if you haven't done your part?" That was the weightiest question I had heard in a long time. It was as if it came directly out of the mouth of God. As soon as I could, I put in the application. Guess what? I was approved. God had already spoken. I had to step out in faith and do my part first. Faith without action is dead.

What has God spoken to you and told you to do? What are you holding back on, thinking that you are waiting on God? What if God is waiting on you? From that lesson, I learned that when God speaks, it will come to pass. God says what He means and means what He says. I learned so much in work-release. I had to make so many right choices to keep living, learning, obeying, and loving God. I had developed a real personal relationship with Jesus Christ. I could not believe the way the Lord, my Lord, had taught me and raised me up, right from the pits of the prison.

My second and final exodus was approaching. I would soon be reunited with my kids. I missed them tremendously. God had given me something that no one could take away. He had given me purpose and taught me how to trust Him.

Most of the time God is telling us to step out of the boat. Trust Him to do the things that we can't do. I was supposed to put in the application. God had already spoken. It is only He who holds the hearts of people in his hands. He turns their hearts whatsoever way that He pleases. The time was finally here for me to go home. Bridges of America had served its purpose in my life. It was now time for me to start this new journey, outside of any prison walls—mentally, spiritually, and physically free—and I was taking Jesus Christ with me.

Purposed-Filled Life

*I have set the Lord always before me: because He is
at my right hand, I shall not be moved.*

— PSALM 16:8

I had set the Lord before me. I was sure nothing that the world had to offer, would move me. I was naked and unafraid before the God that created me, ready to take life on because God had given me a new life. God had given me a reason to live. God had given me purpose. Purpose in Him. Purpose in Christ. From a prison sentence to purpose.

It was August 22, 2019, when I walked out of the gates of Bridges of America, gasping for air, feeling the breeze, and tasting physical freedom. My Gosh! It's been four years since I have been free to just go to a store by myself. Jesus, how free I am!

My kids were awaiting my arrival three hours away in Lake Butler, Florida. I was ready to see them, touch them, hug them, just be around them and my mom. My husband was still in prison. Boy, I surely did miss him. So many emotions were piling up, but I didn't let go of the Hand of God, because I knew I would need Him for the rest of my life.

I finally made it to my kids. What joy welled up in my soul! My goodness, had they grown! They had grown up so much, though my mom hadn't aged a bit. We stayed in Lake Butler, Florida for about seven days before we set off on our new life, my new sober journey, and our new home in Bradenton, Florida. My life was completely different.

God had saved me and turned my life around. I had been found by Jesus.

Sometimes life will throw balls at us that we will miss every single time. I suffered long and hard from the hands of the streets, dibbling and dabbling in drugs, living in the world without a Savior, not having a purpose in this world. I often ask, "How does one learn if there isn't anyone to teach them?" How can a child learn to walk, talk, and function normally without someone there to guide them?

I didn't have guidance. I didn't really have help. Everything I learned, I learned from the streets. Although we had gotten out of Mississippi, I was out on my own by the age of thirteen, learning on my own. Mom did the best that she could. Unfortunately, she could not teach me what she did not know. Often kids grow up without parents which leads them to the streets. Failure creeps in and they continue to search for the feeling of being worthy. Some turn to drugs, some turn to relationships, some turn to violence—but most all of them end up in jail, in prison, or dead.

I look at my own kids today and know that they have to face the fact that both Mom and Dad have been to prison. The statistics are high for them, but Glory be to God that

He has taught us both the most excellent way. God has carried me through, even outside of the prison walls. I knew I could not afford to leave God in prison as some do. No, I needed him every day of my life. I needed him to continue to teach me his ways. To lead me and guide me. I never want to be without Jesus Christ again! I had finally realized why I was created. I was not just made through sex by my mother and father. No, I was created by God with a purpose in mind.

True, most people that serve God in prison will leave him at the gates, but I couldn't—I just couldn't. It is the year 2022 and I am still following God and learning about Him and His ways. I could not imagine life without Him. I see things differently; I make different, healthier choices. I no longer need drugs to mask my pain because Jesus is the best pain reliever I have ever decided to partake in. I am still in awe at the fact that God would want to use an ex-con like myself, yet I accept his call every moment, every day. I answered Him and said, "Yes," to His Will, and "Yes," to His Way—He has not failed me yet, and He never will.

In the eyes of God, you are no different from me. I know times get hard and you feel unworthy or lost or maybe you feel like you have hit rock bottom. Guess what? You are in the perfect place for God to use you. Sometimes we must let go of everything that we thought we knew. Let God pick up us, turn us around, and place our feet on solid ground.

God will call us to let go of everything that has kept us bound, even those things that we don't know we are bound by. Our Father is near those that are broken and bound, those that others put out as outcasts. Those that people assume will be just another crackhead or dope fiend on the street. God specializes in giving purpose to His children that He created. All we must do is seek Him out. I sought Him out and He taught me the good news: The Good news of the gospel.

You may ask, "Well what exactly is the Gospel?" I will stand boldly and say that the Gospel is the absolute truth. The Gospel was preached to me and set my soul free. The Gospel represents the person of Jesus Christ and that He has the power to save souls. I know whom I have believed, and I take Him everywhere I go. The Gospel set me free from me. I accepted the teachings about Jesus as the truth, the whole truth, and nothing but the truth, and that changed my entire life. There is power that overflows about the truth of Jesus. The kind of power that will break you free from any physical or mental prison you may find yourself in. I will never be ashamed to tell the entire world that I met a man that turned my life right side up. I will not be ashamed to tell the world that Christ saved my life. I will not be ashamed to tell the world that I once was lost, but now, I am found.

The thing is this…you must be diligent and serious about your walk with God. Once I was released back onto those streets, everything came at me so fast. My foundation had been laid by God and I was steadfast in my faith, and self-disciplined in His word. I was able to withstand because I was serious about serving the Lord. If God saw fit to meet me in prison knowing all I had done, I was committed to serve him forever. I was dead in my sins, unable to see life as it really was. I only saw what the world showed me, blinded by the lies of Satan.

*And ye shall know the truth, and the truth shall
make you free.*

— JOHN 8:32

But God showed me the *true* truth.

Every single day I still live with the fact that I left my kids, or that I wasn't there for them. I still live with the consequences that come behind all the years I taught my kids the wrong ways to live. I didn't know any other way. I just refuse to get stuck in the woe is me state because I know that the purpose God has is far greater than a prison sentence. Glory to God in the highest. I was not consumed. It was His mercies that kept me. Those same mercies will keep you. God sees you right where you are. His ways are not our ways, nor are His thoughts like ours. God showed me so much kindness and favor in every place my feet touched, and He is still showing me favor now.

We all want to be loved, to be heard, and respected. We all search for our reasons for being here. News flash, the only person that can tell you why you were created is your Creator. If I owned a Ford truck, I can't go to a Chevy dealership to get the manual. Likewise, you can't go to your parents to find out why you were created. Sure, they can tell you what they think your career might look like, but only your Creator can tell you what He created you for, and He created you for a unique purpose. There is a reason you are alive. If you are still breathing, you have purpose.

After everything I been through, it now makes sense. God delivered me from Mississippi. He called me out from among my people because He had set me apart from the foundations of this world. He had a purpose to give me a new heart and a new life so I can go back and set my people free. He had to heal me first. He had to teach me first before He could send me back to redeem anything.

Before He could use me, he had to teach me. There are just some things we are going to have to go through in life because of our upbringings and not having a teacher to guide us. There are just some things we are going to have to endure in this journey so that God can mold us, shape us, and make us fit within His Kingdom. There are some things that we are going to have to shake off because our purpose is greater than our current situations. There are just some things we are going to have to overcome for the purpose of God to lay out across this earth.

God wants to use you in a capacity far greater than what you can see with your natural eyes. The things He has instilled in you is going to make you feel alone. It's going to take you having to be set apart, away from the crowds. You are going to have to say no to a lot of things. Yes, it is going to hurt; the flesh must die. We know death does not feel good; just look at the cross Christ had to carry after getting brutally beaten for us. Yes, Yes, Yes. We, too, will have to bear burdens and die to our own selfish will and desires. When we do, we will see the goodness of God in the land of the living. Glory to God! Hallelujah! I can still praise his name after years of being set free from prison, free from drugs, free from homosexuality, free from mental prison, free from me.

It never feels good to be in the middle of anything, trust me. I know I am now out here walking out my purpose. Your story might not sound like mine, but let me assure you, God can use you. He can use you right where you are today. When you seek Him, and seek Him with your whole heart, He will be found by you. Without Jesus, we are nothing, nor can we do anything apart from Him.

There is hope beyond your circumstances. As I sit and type this today, God has restored my family. My husband and I are reunited. Our kids now have both parents at home, serving the Lord right before their eyes, teaching them the most excellent way. We both serve full-time in the Ministry that God has given to us. I mention all of that to let you know that you can overcome every obstacle that the enemy may try to present to you. Through Christ Jesus, take your eyes off your circumstances and put them on the Lord. You were bought at a price and created to live a purpose-filled life through Christ Jesus.

You see, not only did I enter Gods' Emergency Room, but God also doctored on my husband, right there in prison. We were both serving time at different locations. The power of God met him right where he was. I was praying and praying and believing that if I had to stay married to him, I compelled and cried out to God to save him. I stood on God's word.

> *13 And the woman which hath a husband that*
> *believeth not, and if he be pleased to dwell with*
> *her, let her not leave him.*
> *14 For the unbelieving husband is sanctified by the*
> *wife, and the unbelieving wife is sanctified by*
> *the husband: else were your children unclean;*
> *but now are they holy.*
> *15 But if the unbelieving depart, let him depart. A*
> *brother or a sister is not under bondage in such*
> *cases: but God hath called us to peace.*
> *16 For what knowest thou, O wife, whether thou*

shalt save thy husband? or how knowest thou,
O man, whether thou shalt save thy wife?

— 1 CORINTHIANS 7:13-16

I reminded the Lord of His word, and He honored it. My husband and I were able to correspond with each other while incarcerated, and every chance I got, I would write him and encourage him with scriptures. I spoke of life over my husband, over my marriage, over my family. God honored His word. He saved my husband and set him free, right where he was in prison.

It is amazing how the Spirit of the Living God is not bound by walls, miles, locations, or anything. The Spirit of God blows whichever way it pleases, and no one knows exactly where it has blown.

The wind bloweth where it listeth, and thou hearest
the sound thereof, but canst not tell whence it
cometh, and whither it goeth: so is every one
that is born of the Spirit.

— JOIIN 3:8

But know this: I know His Spirit has blown over my family, my husband, and my life, period.

My husband and I were reckless in the streets, but by God's Grace, we were set free.

*For by grace are ye saved through faith; and that
not of yourselves: it is the gift of God.*

— EPHESIANS 2:8

God was our doctor. He did open heart surgery on both of us. We needed it. We needed it, badly, and God gave us exactly what we needed because we were willing to accept correction. We were willing to look deep within ourselves and be humbled under the mighty Hand of God.

My husband was released from prison seven months after I was released. What a joyous reunion! I hadn't laid eyes on him in five lengthy years; it was long awaited. I drove three-and-a-half hours to pick him up from the Department of Corrections. Tears rolled down my face as I ran into his arms. This time was different though. I finally saw him as the man God had created Him to be. I finally saw purpose for his life. I didn't see him as a drug dealer, a street runner…none of that. I saw him how God saw him as a born-again believer in Jesus Christ.

There is not a soul on this earth that could ever change my mind about God nor the Gospel of Jesus Christ. The Gospel set us free and redeemed our souls.

*For I am not ashamed of the Gospel of Christ: for it
is the power of God unto salvation to every one
that believeth; to the Jew first, and also to the
Greek.*

— ROMANS 1:16

The Gospel gave us purpose and taught us how to live. The Gospel will meet you right where you are. You must be willing to let the ultimate doctor mend your broken heart and save your soul. Step into God's Emergency Room and allow Him to perform open heart surgery on you, all-expenses paid. Undergo His procedure and watch how you heal and come out unblemished, untouched. Free. Healed. Delivered. God saved you on purpose for a purpose.

As I continue to ponder on the goodness of God, I cannot help but continue to praise His name because I know the Almighty God is just waiting on all who will come. He will not turn anyone away.

After being released from prison, I still had to constantly make the right decisions. I no longer found myself in a place where I had nothing but time on my hands. I now have to make the conscious decision to study His work. To pray. To read my Bible. To engage in fellowship with other believers.

God honors that and He continues to honor me outside of the prison walls. He has shown Himself to me, shown Himself faithful even beyond the gates and walls of prison. Jesus continues to lead, guide, and direct my life. He is faithful, even when we are faithless. Oftentimes people "find" God in prison and leave him at the door when released. Of a truth, I could not imagine my life without God. I could not imagine going back into the bondage that the Spirit of Christ released me from.

Make no mistake, there is not a shortage of drugs. There is not a shortage of wrong decisions to be made. But I make the conscious choice to walk by faith, not by sight. I continue to trust in the Lord with all my soul, all my heart, and all of my might. Why? Because I know what He has done for me, just like Joseph. God delivered me from my very own internal prison. I often tell folks that prison is a state of mind. Many days I looked outside the fence during recreation hours and noticed the cars driving by. God spoke to me and told me that most of those folks were physically free, but mentally bound. He told me that I was physically bound, yet spiritually free. Scripture says, "If Jesus sets you free, you are free, indeed" (John 8:36).

Today I boldly and unapologetically walk in that freedom because I know how it feels to be bound in every way possible. I was in bondage to the streets. In bondage to drugs. In bondage to my mind. In bondage to people. But the *Son has set me free* and given me *purpose in Him*.

DEDICATION
to
Ms. Pinkney

Ms. Pinkney was an older lady that had been arrested eleven times and served twelve years in the Department of Corrections. God gave her eyes to see my today. She would leave her dorm to speak life to me, always told me to keep my head up and trust God. She told me I could be free in Prison and be free forever. She was right and I am truly grateful for her sage advice and for her continued positivity. May you be blessed by her guidance.

MRS. PINKNEY'S BEST ADVICE:

✝ Your life doesn't end here, it starts here.

If I have to be here, I must make it count. ✝

✝ Do your time, don't let the time do you, because time is the one commodity you can't get back.

You have a second chance to get it right. ✝

✝ Prison is a state of mind. The Department of Corrections (D.O.C.) was established to correct, so choose to allow the correction to correct.

LETTER
from
Jahkeria Niaza

The following two pages are from my daughter, Jahkeria Niaza, recounting her thoughts and feelings about my time while being incarcerated.

The day my mom went to prison I was really sad for a couple of days. Then, I tried to think... whats going on? why did this happen to her? As the days went by, the weird & sad feelings went away. I knew my mom was going to get out one day, but when? As months went by I wondered when... is she coming home? One day my grandma got a call, it was from my mom, that was the highlight of my day, just to hear her voice. Sadly, years birthdays, christmas, & easter went by without my mom. As the middle child of my mothers, I had to act as the oldest because with out my mom, my two brothers really didn't have an adult to keep them out of trouble & in the streets. As for me, I didn't have anyone to teach me the right things to do. July 4th 2019 came around, that day I made my own count down calender because the next month, the best month I had in 2019, came & it was time for my mom to get out! weeks went by & my mom finally got out. Months went by we were in a new city. I had to relearn my mom because she was a TOTALLY NEW person. From the way she dress to the way she act & believe. I just want to say that I am very proud on her because if she wouldn't have accepted Christ into her life we wouldn't be where we are today. I also want to thank my grandma, Lorraine Johnson, for keeping a roof over our head & making sure we were never starving, even in the hard times she made a way. & more importantly, I want to thank God for never taking his hand & eyes off of us.

PHOTOS
of
My Time in Prison

Although incarcerated in different locations, the SAME GOD met us there in our respectable places by His Spirit. God spoke to us and said wait on Him. He promised to renew our strength and marriage. He did just that; honored His word.

But they that wait upon the Lord shall renew their strength; they shall mount up with wings as eagles; they shall run, and not be weary; and they shall walk, and not faint.

— ISAIAH 40:31

God will honor His Word. I was STILL in prison in this photo, but God is NOT hindered by gates or walls. He brought me out to tell what He has done! He will do the same for you.

Behold, I will do a new thing; now it shall spring forth; shall ye not know it? I will even make a way in the wilderness, and rivers in the desert.

— ISAIAH 43:19

For so long, I thought this was "The Look." Everyone around me got high, so this was my normal. In reality, I was living a silently chaotic lifestyle —dying inside, and nobody knew it but me. I was ashamed of the lifestyle I lived, and it eventually was put on public display.

[20] For when you were slaves of sin, you were free in regard to righteousness. [21] What fruit did you have then in the things of which you are now ashamed? For the end of those things is death.

— ROMANS 6: 20-21

It was time for me to allow the Department to correct me. After-all, I had been found out- God said this is why He ordained Rulers for those that practiced evil, and I my friend practiced evil.

[1]*Let every soul be subject to the governing authorities. For there is no authority except from God, and the authorities that exist are appointed by God. [2]Therefore whoever resists the authority resists the ordinance of God, and those who resist will bring judgment on themselves. [3]For rulers are not a terror to good works, but to evil. Do you want to be unafraid of the authority? Do what is good, and*

*you will have praise from the same. ⁴For he is
God's minister to you for good. But if you do
evil, be afraid; for he does not bear the sword in
vain; for he is God's minister, an avenger
to execute wrath on him who practices evil.*

— ROMANS 13:1-4

FINALLY understood why the women serving LIFE IN PRISON would praise God! Here I was still In Prison, yet FREE.

Let the redeemed of the LORD say so, whom he hath redeemed from the hand of the enemy.

— PSALM 107:2

Sadly we lived in a world with no vision, and lack of knowledge.
We were living in the world with no Savior, nor did we have the
slightest idea that we were perishing. Soon we would go into
captivity.

Therefore my people have gone into captivity,
Because they have no knowledge.

— ISAIAH 5:13

ACKNOWLEDGMENTS
for
Silent Chaos

To God: I thank you for choosing me, delivering me, and setting me free. I will always serve you from a place of gratitude.

To my loving husband, Vertince "Sonny" Green: I love you with everything in me. I thank you for your support and love. I thank God for you. You are my rock under The Rock. The Rock is Jesus Christ. Thank you for being the head of our family. I love you.

To my kids who have endured so much, and still loved me, all the same:

Jahkwon Green: You encourage me more than you know. I love you so much. Always know you can reach any goal you set your mind to.

Jahkeria Niaza: You are always there, willing to jump in and assist me with whatever is needed. You are so smart and talented, and nothing shall by any means stop you. I love you always.

Jashun Green: My character of the three. Son, you always ask me questions that make me think. Continue to reach for the stars, son. You will overcome all that tries to stand in your way. I love you always.

To my mother, Lorraine Johnson: Thank you for not giving up on me when times got hard. You are the strongest woman I know. I love you, always.

To my father, Ernest Ray Womack: Dad, I love you beyond measure, and I would never switch you for anyone else. I love you, and thank you for loving me the best way you knew how.

Sophia, Mrs. Lewis, Mrs. Mitchell, Mr. Lowe, and Mrs. Dexter: thank you for seeing the best in me, despite my Department of Corrections number, J31179.

To my mentors: you all taught me so much, including how to properly speak and become the woman I am today.

To Carol Bear: the artist that hand drew this book cover during our incarceration. Thank you for using your gifts and talents to serve others. You are very talented and made this cover possible. Thank you.

Courtney Jo Barr: May God bless all you put your hands to. We met because my puppy, Milo, ran away and ended up at your house, and from there, God did the rest. From your blunt conversations to the way you are so diligent in business, you have taught me so much. You stayed on me about getting this book completed, now here we are at the finish line. I am grateful for you. Thank you for all you have done.

Karen Salem: As of this day April 28, 2022, I have yet to meet you in person, but I am grateful for you. You stepped up and stepped in to make this book a reality, and I am grateful for you. Thank you so much.

To my counselor, John Patterson: words are too few to express how grateful I am for you. I just want to say thank you, thank you for believing in me, it made a difference in my world, and my children's' world.

To Evangelism Prison Ministry (EE Prison Ministry):
you have no idea how grateful I am for your YES to God!
You came in and allowed God to use you as His instrument
to teach me what to do after my Exodus. To every single
person that has sowed a seed whether financially, their time
or in prayer to this Ministry. *I want you to know; no, I need you
to know.* I am your seed. My family and I, we are forever
grateful for your obedience to Christ Jesus. I thank you, I
thank you, I thank you.

To everyone that has ever spoken love over me…
believed in me… believed in the call God placed over my
life… I just want to say… thank you… thank you…
thank you!

A BLESSING *from the* *Author*

Devoting time to God is a practice that will serve you great purpose in this world. For every situation you will find a Word in The Word that will help you through all trials, tribulations, and misunderstandings. When we set aside time with God through devotional and journaling you are bound to hear The Lord speak to you. It's in those still, quiet moments you can commune with your Father and hear His heart and His will for your life. I encourage you to start this devotional over as often as needed. May God bless you abundantly in your time on communion with Him.

DAILY *Devotional*

Grow in Your Affliction

*But the more they afflicted them, the more they
multiplied and grew. And they were grieved
because of the children of Israel.*

— EXODUS 1:12

Word to the wise
Grow in your affliction
Allow God to multiply you right in the middle of your
affliction
Go throughout this day knowing this,
God is for you, be encouraged.

Sincerely, Hope Regained

My Thoughts . . .

You Were Chosen by Jesus

But God chose the foolish things of the world to shame the wise; God chose the weak things of the world to shame the strong. GOD chose the lowly things of this world and the despised things —and the things that are not—to nullify the things that are.

— 1 CORINTHIANS 27-28

I AM WEAK
I AM FOOLISH
I AM LOWLY
I AM DESPISED
I AM NOTHING

We must be wise enough to know, for these categories are whom God has chosen for himself. You are a child of God.

Sincerely, Hope Regained

My Doodles . . .

God Is Near You

> ¹⁸The Lord is nigh unto them that are of a
> broken heart; and saveth such as be of a
> contrite spirit.
> ¹⁹ Many are the afflictions of the righteous:
> but the Lord delivereth him out of
> them all.
> ²⁰ He keepeth all his bones: not one of them
> is broken."
>
> — PSALM 34: 18-20

Know this, I know that pain runs deep, but I promise you God's love runs deeper, so hold on. Don't give up. Keep the faith in this season.

Sincerely, Hope Regained

My Thoughts . . .

DAY Four
A New Thing

*Behold, I will do a new thing; now it shall spring
forth; shall ye not know it? I will even make a
way in the wilderness, and rivers in the desert.*

— ISAIAH 43:19

God is doing a "new" thing. God is making a way in your
life. It doesn't matter where you are right now. Know this,
God is a man of His word.

Let's thank Him *in advance,*

Sincerely, Hope Regained

My Doodles . . . .

God Moves Mountains

God moves mountains
If you are going through anything…
Fight your battles with praise…
Praise God. Right in the middle of your circumstances, and watch. Him. Move.
Our God will make the "impossible," possible.

Sincerely, Hope Regained

My Thoughts . . .

His Yoke Is Easy

*Come to me, all you who are weary and burdened,
and I will give you rest. Take my yoke upon
you and learn from me, for I am gentle and
humble in heart, and you will find rest for your
souls. For my yoke is easy and my burden is
light.*

— MATTHEW 11:28-30

If you truly know the true truth of God
It is hard to not carry a burden for others
but, in Christ Jesus the yoke is easy and the burden is light
but we must first "come to Him"
He said it in his word

Sincerely, Hope Regained

My Doodles . . .

One Day with Christ

For a day in Your courts is better than a thousand.
I would rather be a doorkeeper in the house of
*   my God*
Than dwell in the tents of wickedness.

— PSALM 84:10

One word from God will change your life and destiny.
It wasn't even what He said that changed my life,
It was the fact that He spoke to me.
God is not a respecter of persons.
Oh Lord, better is one day in your courts
Than a thousand elsewhere.
He counted you worthy.
Thank you, Jesus.

Sincerely, Hope Regained

My Thoughts . . .

Put God First

God is over absolutely everything.
I can't go wrong when putting Him first.
Y'all remember when shades were referred to as "hater
blockers"?
Now, they are just what they are, "sun blockers;" they keep
shade over my pupils when the sun is shining bright.
I don't try to make myself important anymore
by claiming I got haters in the streets.
Man, my life was low-key horrible, who wanted to hate
on me
But, on another note, I have haters in the spirit, and Jesus
serves as my shades.
The true "Son shine" that lit up my soul.
He keeps my haters off.
Satan is my hater,
Jesus said.

If the world hate you, ye know that it hated me
    before it hated you.
If ye were of the world, the world would love his own:
    but because ye are not of the world, but I have
    chosen you out of the world, therefore the world
    hateth you.

—JOHN 15:18-19

Keep your "hater blockers" on.
You have the true Son-shine in my soul.

My Doodles . . . .

DAY Nine
New Mercy From God

²² It is of the Lord's mercies that we are not consumed, because his compassions fail not. ²³ They are new every morning: great is thy faithfulness."

— LAMENTATIONS 3:22-23

It will do you great service to leave yesterday behind. Knowing this, God grants us new mercy every single day. Let's move forward in that with our Hope resting in His word.
God will never leave you nor forsake you.

Sincerely, Hope Regained

My Thoughts . . .

One Way Street

*Jesus saith unto him, I am the way, the truth, and
the life: no man cometh unto the Father, but
by me.*

—JOHN 14:6

We can try to fill the void inside of us with carnal things,
but this I tell you:
There is only One that can fill our soul and feel our
pain, and
There is only One way to Him—that is through Jesus
Christ.
Thank God, He patiently waits on us.
He is our one-way street.

Sincerely, Hope Regained

My Doodles . . . .

Cast Your Cares Upon Him

*Cast thy burden upon the Lord, and he shall
sustain thee: he shall never suffer the righteous
to be moved.*

— PSALM 55:22

God is real.
We have taken on His nature,
Withholding nothing because my life is not my own.
Therefore, I will keep it real in ministry,
Withholding nothing.

Give God your flaws.
Give God your failures.
I gave everything to Him, and told Him to use it as He
pleases.
He will sustain you because He cares for you.

Sincerely, Hope Regained

My Thoughts . . .

DAY Twelve
Heart Condition

> ⁷*But the Lord said unto Samuel, Look not on his countenance, or on the height of his stature; because I have refused him: for the Lord seeth not as man seeth; for man looketh on the outward appearance, but the Lord looketh on the heart.*
>
> — 1 SAMUEL 16:7

Because GOD said it's the condition of the heart that matters to Him,
He does not look at what human eyes can see,
God looks at our heart
Which is desperately wicked.
It is the Spirit of Christ
That changes our hearts,
And, what an awesome surgeon He is.
Are you allowing Him to work on your heart?

Sincerely, Hope Regained

My Doodles . . .

He Woke You Up

If you're reading this, then I want to tell you that you've received your first blessing today!

God woke you up today for a reason.

Now, go and have a blessed and productive day!

And *be a blessing to someone else*

Maybe you are in a confined location and you feel that you are not in a position to bless someone. Let me assure you a gesture as small and simple as calling someone by their real name is a blessing. A simple smile is a blessing. Perhaps a simple heartfelt question such as "How is your day?" can make a difference.

Sincerely, Hope Regained

My Thoughts . . .

DAY
Fourteen
A True Love Story

> *We love him, because he first loved us.*
>
> —1 JOHN 4:19

God loved us first.

> *For God so loved the world, that he gave his only begotten Son, that whosoever believeth in him should not perish, but have everlasting life.*
>
> —JOHN 3:16

He didn't just *"love"* us,
He "so loved us."
Greatest love story ever.

Sincerely, Hope Regained

My Doodles . . . .

God Will Sustain You

*He will not suffer thy foot to be moved: he that
keepeth thee will not slumber.*

— PSALM 121:3

Oh, how awesome it is to know that you are kept by
He who created this world.
God knew you would be right where you are,
He did not suffer you to be moved.
Be encouraged and know
Your Creator sees you.

Sincerely, Hope Regained

My Thoughts . . .

DAY Sixteen
It Is Well

Run now, I pray thee, to meet her, and say unto her,
Is it well with thee? Is it well with thy husband?
Is it well with the child?
And she answered, It is well.

— 2 KINGS 4:26

How awesome is it to be able to stand in the midst of your
circumstances and say, "It is well with my soul."
The blessed assurance that is ours in Christ Jesus.
We know that we know that it is well with our souls,
Because with Jesus, all things are possible.

Sincerely, Hope Regained

My Doodles . . .

DAY
Seventeen
Answer This

*What shall we then say to these things? If God be
for us, who can be against us?*

— ROMANS 8:31

If God is for you,
Who can be against you?
The enemy (Satan) can't stop what's already been ordained
by *God.*
He, *God alone,* gives life, and new days.

Sincerely, Hope Regained

My Thoughts . . .

DAY Eighteen
Freedom

Thank you, Jesus.

I went to prison (physically), and in that prison, I was set *free*. I've been living thirty-three years. Twenty-nine of those years, I was free in the world, but a prisoner of my mind. A prisoner of my circumstances. A prisoner of my past. A prisoner to drugs, alcohol, and money, and in 2016, my body finally caught up with my mental state. My body was thrown into a prison.

So, here I am in a mental AND physical prison. The odds were stacked against me. I failed myself. I failed my mom and dad. And I failed my kids, or so I thought. Then I heard a whisper that the *God* of the Bible could *set me free*.

I jumped on that. I expected Him to overturn convictions, so I stayed at the law library, putting in motion after motion for the first few months. They kept getting denied and I got tired of trying. I gave up. I cried out to God and said, "What do you want from me?"

He said, "I want to save your soul and set you free."

I didn't know anything about a soul, and clearly, I couldn't be set free. *I had already gotten denied*. Sure, I'd heard the word "soul" before. "Soul-food." "Soul-child," words like that, but *never* knew that my soul could be in danger of *Hell, prison, torment,* and *bondage*.

Continuing to study the word of God, I realized that my physical location had absolutely *nothing* to do with my "freedom." In the "Rec Yard," watching the cars pass through the fence, I realized that although people have physical freedom, they could *still* be in prison. Since learning "freedom" is a condition of the spirit and soul, I gave in, and gave my life to *Jesus* in prison.

Jesus set me free, right inside the walls of Gadsden Correctional Facility. He set my *soul* and *spirit* free. I haven't been the same since. Why? Because "He who the Son sets *free* is *free indeed*."

Thank you, *Jesus Christ*.
Not a religion, but a relationship!

My Doodles . . .

DAY
Nineteen
God Is . . .

God is my _______________________________________

God is my _______________________________________

God is my _______________________________________

And still, God is my _______________________________

You fill in the blank_______________________________

He is all I ever need.

My Thoughts . . .

DAY Twenty
No Watered-Down Word

We are losing people *every day*. We don't need to be preaching/teaching a "watered down" Gospel. We need to hear the Truth. We need to hear *Who* can save our souls. I had to hear the *truth*, and it was hard to hear, but that *truth* saved my life. God is *not* a genie in a bottle, nor is He Santa Claus, but *He* sent us *Jesus*. The One who has the power to save souls. My life is *not* perfect. I still have issues, but I *know* if I were to die today, and stand before God, He would let me into His Heaven. Why? Because I have been born again. God is calling us into a real, personal relationship. It's only His grace no one found me dead. It's only His grace I didn't die in a car, plane, train, or walking. It's only His grace I'm not battling cancer. It's only His grace that when I was out in those streets my mother didn't have to bury me. I must give *God* the glory that's due His name.

Sincerely, Hope Regained

My Doodles . . .

Twenty-One
Your Calling

⁴ The Lord God hath given me the tongue of the learned, that I should know how to speak a word in season to him that is weary: he wakeneth morning by morning, he wakeneth mine ear to hear as the learned. ⁵ The Lord God hath opened mine ear, and I was not rebellious, neither turned away back. ⁶ I gave my back to the smiters, and my cheeks to them that plucked off the hair: I hid not my face from shame and spitting. ⁷ For the Lord God will help me; therefore shall I not be confounded: therefore have I set my face like a flint, and I know that I shall not be ashamed.

[8] He is near that justifieth me; who will contend with me? let us stand together: who is mine adversary? let him come near to me. [9] Behold, the Lord God will help me; who is he that shall condemn me? lo, they all shall wax old as a garment; the moth shall eat them up.

— ISAIAH 50:4-9

Sincerely, God

My Thoughts . . .

Twenty-Two
Enemies of God

For if, while we were God's enemies, we were
reconciled to him through the death of his Son,
how much more, having been reconciled, shall
we be saved through his life!

— ROMANS 5:10

We were once enemies of God,
yet God still sent Jesus to die for us so that we can live.

Sincerely, Hope Regained

My Doodles . . . .

DAY Twenty-Three
A Merciful God

I am the LORD;
there is no other God.
I have equipped you for battle,
though you don't even know me,
so all the world from east to west
will know there is no other God.
I am the LORD, and there is no other.
I create the light and make the darkness.
I send good times and bad times.
I, the LORD, am the one who does these things.

— ISAIAH 45: 5-7

The Lord is merciful,
The Scriptures do not lie.
God created light and darkness.
Although God is not in all our thoughts,
Y'all, he has equipped us for battle.

Sincerely, Hope Regained

My Thoughts . . .

Twenty-Four
Waiting Patiently

*That the saying might be fulfilled which He spoke,
"Of those whom You gave Me I have lost none.*

—JOHN 18:9

Jesus is waiting on us. . .
The world has not ended because God is still waiting on some of us to answer the call. Jesus said, "I will not lose any that my father gave me."

God waited on me.

Sincerely, Hope Regained

My Doodles . . . .

DAY
Twenty-Five
Redeemed

Has the LORD redeemed you? Then speak out! Tell others he has redeemed you from your enemies.

— PSALM 107:2 (NLT)

I don't care where I am,
I will bless the Lord at all times.

Sincerely, Hope Regained

My Thoughts . . .

DAY Twenty-Six
Merciful God

Gracious is the LORD, and righteous; yea, our God is merciful.

— PSALM 116:5

God is not fair.
People just ain't fair.
But God is just.
Just refers to an action justified under the circumstances.
Fair refers to an action that treats people as they deserve to be treated.
Many times, actions that are just are not fair.
Stop expecting from other people.
Stop putting expectations on people, period.
Put your expectations in God.
He will never fail you.

Sincerely, Hope Regained

My Doodles . . .

DAY
Twenty-Seven
Hope in God

*I have FULL CONFIDENCE in the things I hope
for, and I am CERTAIN of the things that I
can NOT see.*

— HEBREWS 11:1

I *do not hope* for cars.
I *do not hope* for money.
I *do not hope* for material things.
I know when I seek the kingdom of God
first,
and all his righteousness,
all those "things" will be added to me.

— MATTHEW 6:33

I *do* hope *in God.*

The hope I have is the anchor to my soul. It is sure and steadfast.

— HEBREWS 6:19

I have the mind of Jesus Christ.

— 1 CORINTHIANS
2:16

As is said in Luke 19:10, I do believe the Son of man came to seek and save what was lost.

Jesus saved me.
All my hope is in Jesus.
Once lost, but now I am found.

Sincerely, Hope Regained

My Thoughts . . .

Twenty-Eight
Poem for the Soul

I patiently wait.
What is to come.
What am I destined for?
I no longer want to run.
Surely, if God hadn't stopped me,
I would probably be dead.

I now think back on what my life once was.
Full of lies, deception, money, and drugs.
Full of feelings that portrayed itself as love!

The devil had me completely fooled to think that I wasn't
even committing a crime.
Those are the tricks that the devil plays with our mind.
Look at me now, sitting here doing prison time.

Funny thing is what the devil didn't know.
By me coming to prison, I've had an opportunity to grow.

In this place…
I *literally* had to live out of a box,

But in the midst of it all, God is teaching me the "dos and the do nots."
God has now given me a clear path,
The right way to go.
You see, Satan had stolen my joy,
And turned my life into a circus.

Glory to God, I now know that in *all* things, God works for the good of those who love him and have been called to His purpose.

I said that to say this:
God is a God of multiple chances.
He has given us another chance to get it right.
So, whatever we do,
Let it be pleasing in His sight...

Sincerely, Hope Regained

My Doodles . . .

Twenty-Nine
A Repented Heart

*And the times of this ignorance God winked at; but
now commandeth all men every where to repent.*

— ACTS 17:30

And I did that.
God allowed me to go through my trials and tribulations,
then delivered me so I could be a light for someone else.

Sincerely, Hope Regained

My Thoughts . . .

Love the Lord, Your God

*Jesus replied: "LOVE THE LORD your God with
all your heart and with all your soul and with
all your mind. This is the first and greatest
commandment. And the second is like it: Love
your neighbor as yourself."*

— MATTHEW 22:37-39

Thanking God for waking us up this morning and
screaming,
for this I know.
I can take a pill to put me to sleep,
but y'all, only my God has the power to wake me up.
For that alone,
He deserves my praise.

Jesus has my heart.
Sincerely, Hope Regained

My Doodles . . . .

Free Indeed

If the Son therefore shall make you free, ye shall be free indeed.

— JOHN 8:36

It is hard for a person that is "physically free" to believe they are in prison.
Just like it's hard for a person in "physical prison" to believe they can be free, right where they are.
I am here to tell you that if Christ has made you free, you are free.
Walk in that truth.

Sincerely, Hope Regained

My Thoughts . . .

Thirty-Two
Saved Through Faith

For by Grace you have been saved through faith.
And this is not your own doing; it is the gift
of God.

— EPHESIANS 2:8

If the grace of God covered any of your sins, can I get an
AMEN on this day, y'all?
God granted us His grace as a gift.
Regardless of your background,
God's grace is sufficient.
You have purpose.

Sincerely, Hope Regained

My Doodles . . . .

DAY Thirty-Three
The Struggle Within

*And she will bring forth a Son, and you shall call
His name Jesus, for He will save His people
from their sins.*

— MATTHEW 1:21

August 22, 2019
I was set free, physically.
Since then, at least 10% of the women I was incarcerated
with have overdosed and died.
It seems like every other month I am seeing R.I.P on their
profiles.
At least 10% have returned to prison within just two-and-a-
half years of release.
At least 15% are currently *struggling* with and *fighting*
addiction right now.

Addiction is real, but Jesus is too.
Addiction affects the entire family.
Lord Jesus, here I am.

You see, God doesn't just give you "recovery," He "delivers"
you.

Can a child once delivered from their mother's womb get
back in there?
No!
Delivery is final, recovery is optional.

You can choose to stay clean, but God has a way of totally
delivering you and setting you free.
Thank Jesus.
He delivered me from the snare of the fowler, and the
hands of my enemy.

Pills were the enemy.
Cocaine was the enemy.
Adultery was the enemy.
Lies were the enemy.

But God delivered me from the snare.
Every day we wake up,
God gives us another chance to "wake up."

Sincerely, Hope Regained

My Thoughts . . .

Thirty-Four
Delivered

Smoked so much weed,
My nickname should have been Mary
and my husband's Jane.

It's bad when money and drugs are all you see
To the point that you don't even think.
You are slowly killing people
By putting poison in their bodies.
But, how do you know, if you stayed high yourself.

It's *not enough* to just say *no to drugs*.
They taught me that in school too,
But it didn't work.

Drugs and the streets led us both to prison.
The streets will tell you that's the way to go
The streets will make you sell your own mama crack and
cocaine.
The streets will make you sell your food stamps for drugs,
taking food out of your kid's mouths.
The streets will make your "homeboys" sleep with your

mama, and give her a dime rock because they know she
needs a fix.
The streets will make you get high with your parents; club
with them too.
There ain't no love in the streets, nor in this world, it's only
hate.
That's why Jesus said, "We are in this world, but not of
this world."

The grace of God overtook Sonny Green and me.
Yes, I will always have a memory of these things,
but I remember them with one purpose in mind:
That is to let everyone know, "The streets ain't fa ya."
If God accepted us and wiped us clean,
He can do it for anyone that is willing to ask.
We have kids growing up in this world.
I will forever raise awareness to the schemes of the enemy
and shed light of Jesus Christ, because it is He who
liberated us.

Sincerely, Hope Regained

My Doodles . . .

Thirty-Five
Addicted to the Ministry

If you have ever been addicted to anything, you will understand when I say that I traded my addiction to drugs for another addiction. I am addicted to Christ and to His ministry.

> *I beseech you, brethren, (ye know the house of Stephanas, that it is the first fruits of Achaia, and that they have addicted themselves to the ministry of the saints.)*

> — 1 CORINTHIANS 16:15

P.S. You see, God knows how to speak my language. He knows that I know what it means to be addicted to something. Therefore, He knows that I understand the same way I was bold, tenacious, fierce, and eager to go after those drugs. That's how I am for His Kingdom.

Sincerely, Hope Regained

My Thoughts . . .

DAY Thirty-Six
No Never

Jesus, I will never forget how you set me free.

Jesus, I will never forget how you brought me out.
Jesus, I will never forget, not ever!

God used a four-year prison sentence to save my life.
He, alone, turned it around for his good (Romans 8:28).

From drug addict, to being set free by Jesus!

Jesus accepted me dressed in a blue uniform.
In a place that didn't call me by name, but by J31179.

No one could ever change my mind about my Lord!

Sincerely, Hope Regained

My Doodles . . .

Thirty-Seven
Hey Y'all

Therefore if any man be in Christ, he is a new creature: old things are passed away; behold, all things are become new.

— 2 CORINTHIANS 5:17

That is it.
That is all.

Sincerely, Hope Regained

My Thoughts . . .

Thirty-Eight
God Ordained the System

Serving time in prison.... I realized I couldn't "Fix the system!!!!!"

So, I stopped trying to fix it, and asked God to feed me there.

Feed me HIS FOOD...

He did, I realized.

I was broken.

The "power" the system had was ordained by God.

> *Let every soul be subject unto the higher powers. For there is no power but of God: the powers that be are ordained of God.*
>
> — ROMANS 13:1

Sometimes, we have to take our eyes off of our circumstances and turn them inwards.

God fed me, fixed me, *and* set me free, right in the system!

I decided to allow the Department of Correction to correct me.

I decided to allow God to correct me.

I was released from prison in 2019
I was no longer dancing with the devil!
God knew I would be there before I was even born.
He also knew when He would bring me out!
I was gonna ride with Him.

Sincerely, Hope Regained

My Doodles . . .

Thirty-Nine
Beauty for Ashes

To give unto them beauty for ashes,
The oil of joy for mourning, the garment of praise
for the spirit of heaviness.

— ISAIAH 61:3

God has truly given me "Beauty for Ashes."

I used to use makeup to make up my happiness.
I used beauty products to hide the hurt and ugliness inside,
but *Jesus* has set me free.

Sincerely, Hope Regained

My Thoughts . . .

Shackles on My Feet

"Johnson, lower bunk, pack it up."

"Johnson for transport."

I laid there crying, afraid and not ready to face reality.

The time had come for me to be transferred from Duval County Jail, Jacksonville, Florida to Lowell Correctional Facility in Ocala, Florida.

I finally got up after the guard walked to my bunk and made me.

I remember the sound of the shackles on my feet.

I remember the sounds of the shackles around my wrists!

Crying.

Afraid.

Ashamed.

Plain out broken, I was.

They loaded us on the bus. There were around ten women of all races, sizes, and ages, yet I felt like this was only happening to me.

This was one of the longest rides of my life.

I didn't know what to expect.

We arrived at our destination, exited the bus, and waited for forever.

Finally, they made us strip down, gave us shampoo, had to bathe in cold water.
Then we had to bend over, cough and squat.
So degrading to me.
After that was completed, I will never forget looking up at the guard and hearing them say, "Keep your head down and don't look any officer in the eye."
I will end it right there.
I took that statement to heart. I would walk around the compound with my head held down, fear of getting in trouble and the guards doing something to me.
Lowell was a beast.
One day, I heard one of the visitors that came to speak in the Chapel.
It was my first time really hearing the Gospel and that Jesus loved me, in spite of *me*.
Slowly, GOD began to remove the shame.
Remove the pain.
Remove the guilt.
Slowly, my head began to raise because I knew I was forgiven by God.
Today, I walk unashamed and unapologetic with my head held high, spreading the same love, hope, and Jesus that someone spread to me.
Listen, I don't care where you are, but know this: Jesus has the power to meet you there, heal, and deliver you so that your story, failures, and shortcomings will be a testimony to others.

Sincerely, Hope Regained

My Doodles . . .

Forty-One
Enlarge My Territory

When you pray the Jabez prayer,
Asking God to "Enlarge your territory,"
Just because your face is *not* on a big screen, does not mean
He has not answered.
Look around you.
Any new faces?
If so, work that field, because if you prayed,
God answered.
He who is faithful in little will be faithful with much.

> *And Jabez called on the God of Israel saying, "Oh,
> that You would bless me indeed, and enlarge my
> territory, that Your hand would be with me, and
> that You would keep me from evil, that I may
> not cause pain!"*
>
> —1 CHRONICLES 4:10

So, God granted him what he requested.

Sincerely, Hope Regained

My Thoughts . . .

Forty-Two
Can You Relate?

In prison I sat on my bunk.
Took a staple and used it as a needle.
Crushed down pencil lead that I used for ink.
I attached the staple to a pencil and went to work.
I sat there and cut letters into my skin that spelled out
"death."
Thing is, almost everyone around me did it too.
People called it talented.
Today, I call it insanity because not once did I think about
lead poisoning.
I didn't think about penetrating my skin.
I didn't think at all.
That demon kept me in the tomb, cutting myself.
But, then I read Mark 5:
"And always, night and day, he was in the mountains and in
the tombs, crying out and cutting himself with stones."
You see, I was out of my mind like him.
But when I read verse 6: "When he saw Jesus from afar, he
ran and worshiped Him." I, too, saw Jesus.
I couldn't take back the outer scars I gave myself because
tattoos are meant to be permanent.

But, my inner scars, Jesus healed.
Jesus healed my mind, y'all.
Jesus kept me sane during my moments of insanity.

Sincerely, Hope Regained

My Doodles . . .

Ordained By God

I have set my rainbow in the clouds, and it will be the sign of the covenant between me and the earth.

—GENESIS 9:13

The rainbow will always signify the covenant and promise
of God
God is amazing.
God is love.
His ways are perfect, and His words are true.
The rainbow was and is ordained by God as a sign to us as
a promise from Him. The rainbow could never be a sign
that homosexuality is okay, for I used to be homosexual
until Jesus Christ set me free.

*[26]Because of this, God gave them over to shameful
lusts. Even their women exchanged natural
sexual relations for unnatural ones. [27] In the
same way the men also abandoned natural
relations with women and were inflamed with*

lust for one another. Men committed shameful acts with other men and received in themselves the due penalty for their error.

— ROMANS 1:26-27

192

Be careful not to make light of that which God ordained.

Sincerely, Hope Regained

My Thoughts . . .

Forty-Four
God Considered a Nobody

I am so grateful that God loves the ones that the world considers a "nobody."

> *The Lord did not set his love upon you, nor choose you, because you were more in number than any people; you were the fewest of all people: But because the Lord loved you, and because he would keep the oath which he had sworn unto your fathers, hath the Lord brought you out with a mighty hand, and redeemed you out of the house of bondmen.*
>
> — DEUTERONOMY 7:7-8

You are the fewest.
You are redeemed.
God has chosen you.
Yes, you.

Sincerely, Hope Regained

My Doodles . . . .

Forty-Five
Speak, Testify, Speak

For if you remain silent at this time, relief and
deliverance for the Jews will arise from another
place, but you and your father's family will
perish. And who knows but that you have come
to your royal position for such a time as this?

— ESTHER 4:14

I was once told "You have the right to remain silent," and
I did.
But, in the case of the Gospel, I don't have the "right," but I
do have a "choice."
So, in this case, I'm a witness to the truth.
I will be an Esther. I'm going to the King on behalf of my
people
Who knows if God brought you in for "such a time as
this?"

Sincerely, Hope Regained

My Thoughts . . .

Naked and Afraid

> And she called the name of the Lord that spake unto
> her, Thou God seest me: for she said, Have I
> also here looked after him that seeth me?

— GENESIS 16:13

I spent years hiding because I was naked and afraid.

> And the LORD God called unto Adam, and said
> unto him, Where art thou?
> And he said, I heard thy voice in the garden, and I
> was afraid, because I was naked; and I hid
> myself.

— GENESIS 3:9-10

Not knowing that God saw me anyways,
He saw me naked and afraid, and covered me in sheep's
clothing, and drowned my fears in the blood of the lamb,
Christ Jesus.
Thank God, He saw me anyways.

My Doodles . . .

Forty-Seven
Walking with God

Walking with God I have learned this:
He will show *you* the "good" and the "bad"
Once He shows you, He expects you to change it and live up to it.
The "bad," He expects you to correct; the "good," He expects you to live up to.

God has used so many people to show me the gifts that have been "untouched" within me. But He has assured me that they are there.
Now,He says, live it and activate the gifts I have bestowed upon you
He gives us gifts, and talents to edify others.
Okay, God… once again, I surrender.

Sincerely, Hope Regained

My Thoughts . . .

Forty-Eight
Do Your Part

When we want God to move, we *always* have to do our part.

> ⁷*Ask and it will be given to you; Seek and you will find; Knock and the door will be opened to you. ⁸For everyone who asks receives; the one who seeks finds; and to the one who knocks, the door will be opened.*

> — MATTHEW 7:7-8

It doesn't matter how long my puppy Milo sits at the kids' room door. If he doesn't scratch the door to let them know he is there, it will not open.

He can't just sit there; he must do his part.

As it is with us—we can't just sit still and wait on God to move. He requires us to do our part. Faith without action is dead.

How can you receive without asking?

How can we find without seeking?

How will the door open without us knocking?

Let's not be like Milo.
Start asking, seeking, knocking, and God will do his part.
Be blessed, and be a blessing.
Lord, we thank you for your word.

Sincerely, Hope Regained

My Doodles . . .

Forty-Nine
Check His Track Background

Go ahead,
Google me.
Check my track record.
It will tell you of my "background."
Now, go ahead,
read the word of God.
Check His track record.
His word will tell you of His background and what he Has promised.

> ^{2}And I will make of thee a great nation, and I will
> bless thee, and make thy name great; and thou
> shalt be a blessing:
> ^{3} And I will bless them that bless thee and curse
> him that curseth thee: and in thee shall all
> families of the earth be blessed.

— GENESIS 12:2-3

Oftentimes, there is a "delay" between God's promises and their fulfillment.

Abraham was promised descendants years before Isaac's birth.

There were 25 years between Joseph's dreams and the time his brothers and father bowed before him in Egypt (Genesis 37:2, 41:46, 53).

David was a teenager when Samuel anointed him the next King of Israel, but he was thirty when he actually began his reign.

There were four hundred years between God's promise of a Messiah and Jesus' birth.

We might see these things as a delay, but know this:

Not one word will fail (Joshua 21:45.)

I believe God for me.

I believe Him for you too.

Sincerely, Hope Regained

My Thoughts . . .

Without Honor

> *But Jesus said unto them, A prophet is not without*
> *honour, but in his own country, and among his*
> *own kin, and in his own house.*

— MARK 6:4-6

Isn't that Mary and Joseph's son?
Isn't He the carpenter's son?
Jesus' own brother didn't believe in Him, but that didn't
stop Him from accomplishing his purpose for which God
had called Him.
Well, Maria, how do you know?

Because of Mark 6:5:
"And he could there do no mighty work, except
that he laid his hands upon a few sick folk and
healed them."

There were a few that had enough faith in Him to get their
healing.

Those "few" were ones who God had sent for Him there in the first place; those who believed in Him.
The moral of this story is that not everyone is called to you.
Everyone is not going to believe in you.
God will use the hands and hearts of strangers to accomplish His purpose.
Most of the time, folks are waiting on God to prove Himself to them,
and that is just what God wants to do, so they cannot say they played a part in what God has done.

Be patient in Christ!
Be resilient in Christ!
Be obedient to God!
Be available for God!

Sincerely, Hope Regained

My Doodles . . .

Fifty-One
Able and Willing

*She seeketh wool and flax, and worketh willingly
with her hands.*

— PROVERBS 31:13

Working willingly.
I am She.
Regained Hope.
Gideon Season.

Sincerely, Hope Regained

My Thoughts . . .

Fifty-Two
Wages of Sin Is Death

*For the wages of sin is death, but the gift of God is
eternal life in Christ Jesus our Lord.*

— ROMANS 6:23

You know how we work for our "wages" today on our jobs.
When payday comes, they "*better*" have that check, right?
And give us what we deserve and/or worked for, right?
I am grateful God did not. I said "*do not*" give me what I
deserved, because I am a born sinner and the wages of sin
is death.
Then there is the "but."
We all should be grateful for the "buts" in the Bible because
after the "but" is where we find grace and mercy.
Thank you, Jesus, for You.

Sincerely, Hope Regained

My Doodles . . .

Fifty-Three
I Love the Lord Because

One reason I love Jesus Christ is because He died for me.
One reason I love God is because when I needed someone the most, He was there.
God lifted my head, y'all, when I was at my lowest, and nursed me to health.
I will forever serve Him with my life.

> *3 But you, Lord, are a shield around me,*
> *my glory, the One who lifts my head high.*
> *4 I called out to the Lord,*
> *and he answers me from his holy mountain.*
> *5 I lie down and sleep;*
> *I wake again, because the Lord sustains me.*
> *6 I will not fear though tens of thousands*
> *assail me on every side.*

— PSALM 3:3-6

My shield.
Lifter of my head.
Sustainer.
My God.

Sincerely, Hope Regained

My Thoughts . . .

Fifty-Four
Made Perfect in Weakness

"Jesus loves me, this I know,
for the Bible tells me so. . ."

We love him, because he first loved us.

—1 JOHN 4:19

Back to the basic simple truth.

"Little ones to Him belong,
they are weak, but He is strong. . ."

But he said to me, "My grace is sufficient for you,
for my power is made perfect in weakness.

—2 CORINTHIANS 2:9

Yes, Jesus loves me and you.
It is a simple truth.

Sincerely, Hope Regained

My Doodles . . .

Fifty-Five
Run Harder

Y'all, when I ran with the enemy, Satan, I ran hard. I broadcasted my life. Now, I run even harder with my friend, father, healer, provider, protector, and King, Jesus, and I'm going to tell the world.

Making moves with Christ:

> *Let us lay aside every weight, and the sin which doth so easily beset us, and let us run with patience the race that is set before us.*

> — HEBREWS 12:1

Sincerely, Hope Regained

My Thoughts . . .

Nothing Is Too Hard for God

Lord, I just can't get you off my mind. Fall fresh on me. God is waiting to heal minds, hearts, relationships, finances, souls—all you have to do is say, "Yes!"

There is nothing too hard for the Lord.

Big facts.

Sincerely, Hope Regained

My Doodles . . .

Fifty-Seven
Pleasing to God

*Let the words of my mouth, and the meditation of
my heart, be acceptable in thy sight, O Lord,
my strength, and my Redeemer.*

— PSALM 19:14

Sincerely, Hope Regained

My Thoughts . . .

Power to Save

My goodness, only the *Lord* had enough *power* to save me because I was killing myself. I will continue to share with any and everyone what *Jesus* has done for me. He set me free. I am unashamed of what the *Lord* has done.

Sincerely, Hope Regained

My Doodles . . .

Fifty-Nine
God Grants Us Grace

> But The Lord said to Samuel, "Do not consider his appearance or his height, for I have rejected him. The Lord does not look at the things people look at. People look at the outward appearance, but the Lord looks at the heart.
>
> —1 SAMUEL 16:7

This one hits me every time.
God granted me grace, y'all.
I was coked up, pilled up, and dead in the streets, but God looked at my heart
and He chose me when I was in my mess, because God doesn't look at what we look at.

My Thoughts . . .

DAY
Sixty
Trust Him

[5]*Trust in the Lord with all thine heart; and lean
not unto thine own understanding.*
[6]*In all thy ways acknowledge him, and he shall
direct thy paths.*
[7]*Be not wise in thine own eyes: fear the Lord and
depart from evil.*
[8]*It shall be health to thy navel, and marrow to thy
bones.*
[9]*Honor the Lord with thy substance, and with the
first fruits of all thine increase.*

— PROVERBS 3:5-9

Sincerely, Hope Regained

My Doodles . . .